iOS Wow Factor

Apps and UX Design Techniques
for iPhone and iPad

Timothy Wood

Apress®

iOS Wow Factor

ISBN-13 (pbk): 978-1-4302-3879-9

ISBN-13 (electronic): 978-1-4302-3880-5

President and Publisher: Paul Manning
Lead Editors: Steve Anglin and Tom Welsh
Technical Reviewer: Adam Smith
Editorial Board: Steve Anglin, Mark Beckner, Ewan Buckingham, Gary Cornell, Morgan Ertel, Jonathan Gennick, Jonathan Hassell, Robert Hutchinson, Michelle Lowman, James Markham, Matthew Moodie, Jeff Olson, Jeffrey Pepper, Douglas Pundick, Ben Renow-Clarke, Dominic Shakeshaft, Gwenan Spearing, Matt Wade, Tom Welsh
Coordinating Editor: Kelly Moritz
Copy Editor: Lawrence Hargett
Compositor: Apress Production (Christine Ricketts)
Indexer: SPI Global
Illustrator: Timothy Wood
Artist: SPI Global
Cover Designer: Anna Ishchenko

Distributed to the book trade worldwide by Springer Science+Business Media, New York, 233 Spring Street, 6th Floor, New York, NY 10013. Phone 1-800-SPRINGER, fax (201) 348-4505, e-mail orders-ny@springer-sbm.com, or visit www.springeronline.com.

For information on translations, please e-mail rights@apress.com, or visit www.apress.com.

Apress and friends of ED books may be purchased in bulk for academic, corporate, or promotional use. eBook versions and licenses are also available for most titles. For more information, reference our Special Bulk Sales–eBook Licensing web page at www.apress.com/bulk-sales.

Contents

About the Author

Tim Wood is currently Director of User Experience at EffectiveUI, where he leads an award winning design team specializing in the creation of custom applications for the web, mobile, and desktop environments.

For more than a decade, Tim has persistently focused on the radical transformation of business through user experience. From next-generation consumer electronics to highly specialized mobile applications, his passion for design has fueled an inherent desire to innovate and promote progressive methods of interaction design. Tim holds an MFA in Computer Graphics and Interactive Media Development from the Rochester Institute of Technology and is an internationally recognized speaker on the topics of user experience design, user interface design and interaction design.

Tim lives in upstate New York with his partner Lynne, their cat Elysium and a random assortment feral cats and other urban wildlife. When not designing, Tim can usually be found bounding quickly and quietly through the forests of the northeast on his mountain bike… only getting out of hand and crashing some of the time.

About the Technical Reviewer

Adam Smith is a Rochester Institute of Technology Associate Professor and chairs its New Media Design program in the College of Imaging Arts and Sciences (CIAS). He has led key efforts to incorporate industry collaboration in the department's undergraduate design education. Graphics Live Magazine, Graphic Design USA, STC conferences, and Adobe.com have all featured this focus and the interactive design, user experience, and cross-device-development educational processes he initiated at RIT. The New Media Program has helped create an award winning and internationally recognized design program at RIT.

Acknowledgments

It would be a tough task to call out everyone who influenced the thinking expressed here in this book. There's been an endless stream of collaborators, colleagues, instigators, and sounding boards that have helped me understand my own perspective on user experience design. However, for their early insight and influence in my more formative years I would like to thank Wayne Neale, Chris Koch, Corey Bernardo, and Mike Telek.

I would also like to thank Lucas Jordan for helping make this book possible.

Special thanks goes to Lynne Mikel for her unwavering support while this book was being written.

Introduction

It's a tough market out there, and as I'm sure you know, it can be very difficult for your application to get noticed in the App Store. There are literally hundreds of thousands of both interesting and not so interesting applications available for download now. Just having a highly functional and stable application from a development perspective isn't enough to get your app the recognition it needs to go mainstream. Users expect to be 'Wowed' with their iOS apps, this is probably something that you have experienced yourself. As you probably know, it's the 'Wow Factor' of that initial app experience that sets the hook and gets users engaged with the features and functions that you or your development team have been working so hard to create. It's 'Wow Factor' that gets you world of mouth recommendations between friends and great reviews in the app store. It's 'Wow Factor' that can drive the viral adoption of the application that ends up funding your early retirement! The big question is, what is Wow Factor, and how do you get it?

Those are not easy questions to answer, but the good news is that there are answers, and I certainly will address those later in this book - but you need to know that you can get to 'Wow' if you are willing to start paying close attention to the details of your application experience. There's no doubt about it, critical thinking, excellent problem solving skills, and solid design methods are behind any great user experience. Elevating your design practice to a higher level is absolutely necessary to get that 'Wow' that you are looking for, and that's at the heart of what this book is about. But 'Wow' takes more than good design practice. It's also rooted in how you think about, or frame up your design problems and that requires a greater understanding of the wider context for the design decisions you are going to make.

It's my firm belief that you can't truly know where you are going without a good understanding of where you have been. The iPhone isn't the first smartphone to appear in the market, although it is one of the most success-ful and influential. As an application designer, or developer, you understand at some level the huge opportunity this new platform presents and obvious-ly you'd like to take advantage of it. By looking into the past we can under-stand why the iPhone is the way it is and why it is held up as a shining bea-con of great user experience.

As you think about your application, you may need to build upon some of the fundamental concepts behind that experience the core experience of iOS, but on the other hand, you may just want to toss them aside. The idea behind this book is fairly simple, to give you, designer and developer, prac-tical insights into the nature of the iOS user experience, while empowering you with information to create your own exceptional applications. For many people, Apple's Human Interface Guidelines is the starting point for under-standing the possibilities that iOS enables for users. But what do you do if you need to go beyond those rudimentary guidelines? Because they are just that, rudimentary - and that's just not going to cut it for you! This book intends to help push you beyond the basic assumptions you may have about iOS applications provide you with the ideas and techniques that will help you build upon your own insights and free your personal creativity.

Creating a successful iOS application isn't easy, but it's my hope that this book will help you take your application to the next level and help it get the attention that it deserves.

Putting the iOS Human Interface Guidelines in Context

Apple's iOS Human Interface Guidelines (HIG) aim to be the definitive starting point for designers and developers new to the platform. The company's approach to the guide is simple—provide a critical mass of information, techniques, and basic methods to get an individual or development team building applications as quickly as possible.

The guidelines set out to make the reader aware of the radically new interaction model that the platform presents. The initial challenge for Apple, when the device was opened up for third-party application development, was to get the platform adopted as a viable vehicle for the distribution and deployment of applications.

At the time of Apple's App Store launch in the summer of 2008, there was a well-established community of specialized teams focused on mobile devices and consumer electronics that were well-positioned to migrate to this platform and to begin creating software for it. However, the skills and expertise required for success were still considered a relatively niche domain. Apple needed a much broader base of development teams populating the App Store with great software in order for their strategy to succeed.

Looking Back

Before 2008, mobile applications were a somewhat primitive affair—at least by today's standards. This was not due to any lack of trying on the part of developers; it was because of the technological limitations imposed by devices. "Feature phones" of the era were known for their portability, with small size being among the top criteria for success. Subsequently, these devices had very small displays with both low bit-depth color support and low resolution for their scale. Processor capability and memory availability were other significant constraints. This meant that the design of a mobile application was an exercise in minimalism and restraint. In that environment, the expectations for what a mobile application could be, how it would work, and what it looked like were not very high. Market fragmentation presented its own set of challenges as well, driving designers and developers to target a lowest common denominator of input and display to ensure success across a large variety of devices. This approach contributed significantly to a suboptimal user experience for applications running on those devices.

"Smartphones" presented a different set of challenges. They usually had larger, higher-quality screens and much greater computational capacity. However, these devices often had unique input characteristics that varied significantly from manufacturer to manufacturer. Some of the more prevalent forms of input included

- Jog dials
- Four- and five-way controllers
- Dedicated buttons or hard keys
- Variable buttons or soft keys
- Stylus input
- Touch input

A given device incorporated any combination of these controls as a part of its design. In many cases the nature of the input was considered a "signature interaction" from which a device's particular brand could be identified. Much of this was due to the fact that most early smartphones were a direct evolution from the popular PDAs (personal digital assistants) that preceded them. So naturally, these new types of phones inherited those interaction characteristics in order to leverage the value and recognition of the signature interaction.

With the maturation of the feature phone and smartphone markets, there was a high degree of specialization and focus surrounding the design and development of software for those devices. Fragmentation of the smartphone market and the idiosyncrasies of each platform pushed that knowledge into increasingly esoteric enclaves of design practice.

Apple's iPhone challenged those expectations. Previously held beliefs about what a mobile phone was, what it could do, and how it could operate needed to change radically, so individuals with previous domain expertise needed to be prompted to change their mindsets.

We take devices like the iPad and iPhone for granted now, but we have to remember that when the iPhone was originally released there was some controversy about the Home button and the phone's general form factor. The simplicity of the device, its large screen (at the time), and lack of dedicated hard controls were in stark contrast to virtually all other smartphones of the day. People immediately questioned the functionality and usability of the Home button. Some even thought that the success of the product hinged on that single control. The migration of many controls from dedicated hard buttons to pixels displayed on the touch screen were also a significant point of contention.

It's through that lens that we begin to understand the nature of the HIG. We can see that history reflected in two main themes that emerge when reviewing the documentation:

- Understanding the platform implications, particularly around input and control, including the passive sensing capabilities

- Awareness and sensitivity to well-executed user experience in the context of the platform's technical capabilities and physical attributes

Essentially, this is the purpose of the "Platform Characteristics" section of the HIG, which makes a number of points intended to ease teams into understanding how different this platform is from what they may have worked on in the past.

This was necessary because without eliminating the preconceived notions of the industry at that time, it would not have been possible to achieve the level of execution the device required. This was a sensible approach for Apple, as it reinforced the strategy of establishing the device as a mainstream platform with mass-market appeal.

Limitations

However, the HIG has its drawbacks and limitations. While Apple is careful to delineate Human Interface Principles and User Experience Guidelines, both of these areas are somewhat limited in scope. Interaction designers may not find much value in these sections owing to the concrete nature of the statements made there; the lack of abstraction or underlying rationale behind the recommendations provides little on which interaction designers can build. The design content of the document is thus too general, lacking the depth to empower sophisticated user experience design activities.

The HIG also makes some perfunctory statements about process that are clearly targeted toward less-experienced teams, and while the process statements are valid for certain scenarios, they don't provide a clear understanding of a comprehensive design methodology that can be adapted to many needs and situations.

The limitations are not necessarily problematic for a first attempt at creating a good or even great iOS application, given the nature of the target audience. The fact that Apple has prioritized display size, display orientation, and the dynamics of capacitive touch screen interface input tells us that they are intent on democratizing mobile application (and mobile web) expertise by having design and development teams focus on input and output as the most important factors for understanding a user interface solution.

We can't expect Apple to provide an all-inclusive resource for creating great software. The HIG is an excellent starting point, but if we take a step back we can see that it is really about addressing the risks of opening up the device to third-party developers—protecting Apple's brand image and perception of iOS devices within the market to ensure their continuing success. Apple is completely justified in having ulterior motives since the success of any given third-party application becomes a success for their organization. By outward appearances it seems that Apple is trying to democratize good design, but the HIG also aims to preserve and perpetuate the brand through the following strategy:

- Creating a sense of exclusivity and cultural cachet for consumers

- Maintaining the aspirational aura associated with iOS devices and the brand itself

- Justifying premium pricing within a market known for its razor-thin margins

- Of course, this should not be a surprise to anyone, but we should recognize that these are some of the fundamental driving factors of the iOS Human Interface Guidelines.

Beyond the HIG

Successful mobile applications require more than a basic understanding of user experience and design-related issues. Now that a few generations of iOS applications have cycled through the market, it is important to define and document concrete information related to the development of compelling device interaction and how that can work to establish the right level of competitive differentiation for a particular software product. And beyond the basic "Aesthetic Integrity" outlined by the HIG, how can creating impactful visual experiences contribute to the compelling device interaction and the differentiation you may be striving for? These are issues that are not fully addressed—at least not at a level that is easy to understand.

This book intends to dive a bit deeper into the mechanics of iOS to help you understand the methods and techniques that can be employed to move beyond a basic application. I will bypass any argument for or against custom controls and show you the tools and tactics required to design an amazing application from scratch, or undertake the wholesale reinvention of an existing application.

The topics covered in depth later in this book are more concerned with the mechanics of compelling interaction that will ultimately make people love your software. Classic or more typical usability themes will be approached from this perspective as well. However, you should understand that while classic usability concepts are fundamental to successful software, in some cases it may be necessary to set different priorities when designing for "desire." The impact of those types of design choices will be reviewed in an effort to give you an understanding of what's in the balance when trying to make the right decision.

You should already have some familiarity with the HIG as well as some experience designing, specifying, or building apps for either the iPhone or the iPad. A working knowledge of user experience design practice, or at least some degree of exposure to that type of thinking is assumed as well. However, if that's not the case, you still will find value in this book and have at your disposal the means to develop the concepts that will elevate your iOS app and engender a sense of Wow! with your users.

Deconstructing the iOS User Experience

It is important to recognize that it's not a single design element or interaction that makes the iOS user experience so successful and popular. All user experience can be expressed as a gestalt effect. In other words, that which we experience is greater than the qualities of the individual components we perceive. You can't truly understand what it is about iOS (and subsequent applications) that makes it so attractive without pulling it apart piece by piece. So let's take a deeper look into iOS and break down some of the fundamental elements of user experience that define the nature of the operating system and the fundamental framework of iOS applications.

The first part of this deconstruction will focus on higher-level issues including the presentation metaphor, the concept of direct manipulation, and the centrality of the Home button. Later on I will break down some of the interaction mechanics inherent to all iOS applications in terms of their presentation and the mental model that presentation suggests for users. Beyond that,

I'll look at some of the core philosophy behind iOS and how that philosophy is applied, and even how that philosophy is often contradicted or ignored. And finally, I'll cover the aesthetic components of the experience and explain how visual design can provide the continuity that pulls all of these disparate elements together.

Metaphor vs. Utility

One of the more interesting aspects of the iOS experience is how the OS layer of the device fundamentally lacks a visual metaphor. The fact that this was never an obstacle to the perceived usability of the iPhone when it was initially released tells us a lot about the changing nature of users over the past decade or so. As stated earlier, there was some consternation regarding the physical design of the device, and the inclusion of a single hard control for operating the user interface (UI). This is a clear indicator of a fairly conservative view of the media, and likely the populace at large too. So why didn't the on-screen user interface result in a negative reaction? It was a departure from preceding devices, and it certainly did not have a clear relationship to desktop UIs.

The key to understanding the success of the iPhone UI lies in recognizing the emphasis the design places on utility, rather than metaphor. Why was this decision made? Apple had already revolutionized personal computing with the metaphor-rich graphical user interface, a design solution that played a fundamental role in the rapid adoption of the PC. Highly accessible ideas like "desktop," "files," and "folders," and their representation within a graphical framework that you could see and interact with directly, are now ingrained in our communal consciousness. A departure from a highly metaphorical interaction model was not necessarily a deliberate move when you look at the iPhone in comparison to its contemporaries at the time of its release. Smartphones and feature phones already had a well-established design ethos that evolved from the increasing complexity of their functionality—an increasing number of features and an increasingly sophisticated means by which to navigate those features. In many cases this evolution resulted in a matrix of icons navigated by some kind of four-way control. This is a very utilitarian approach to the design of a UI. One quickly scans a screen for the appropriate function for the task at hand, selects that function, and executes the task. Speed and efficiency are the determining factors here, and there is very little tolerance to complex metaphorical environments that must first be deciphered by the user.

iOS devices are no different. There is a lack of overt or overarching visual metaphor at the OS layer, yet at the same time it is still very graphical in nature. What we need to recognize is that at the root level of the OS, the user is presented with an inherently abstract space populated with button-like controls that represent the applications available on the device. Some of these controls contain artwork that is minimal and iconic, while others are very rich and illustrative. Sometimes the artwork is representative of the underlying functionality and sometimes it is not. Beyond the basic geometry that bounds them, the icons' only shared characteristics are a few minor rendering attributes that give the user an indication that these controls may be touchable. In most cases, a user will first identify an app icon by its visual appearance. Reading the app icon's label is entirely a secondary action. This behavior becomes very evident when swiping through multiple screens of applications; a user must quickly scan the screen before making the decision to swipe again. The simplistic presentation model at the OS level becomes usable when it is enabled by the visual nature of the app icons.

There is no notion of a file system on iOS devices, which reinforces the non-metaphorical approach. If there is no desktop and no folders, then the concept of files certainly becomes a very difficult concept to manage. Content types are dealt with in a very unambiguous manner—they run seamlessly as part of the application workflow that led to their creation or discovery. The user isn't burdened with having to organize files within a file system hierarchy, and subsequently having to find or search for those files when they are needed again. Each application manages its relevant "content objects" in its own way. The nature of the content object often defines the method of organization and browsing interaction for the user. Here are a few examples of apps, their content types, and their method of organization:

- Camera: Camera Roll: image array or one-up swipe-able browsing

- iPod: List-based media object browsing or carousel browsing

- iBooks: Library: book/document array or list-based browsing

There are numerous other examples that I could point to as well. And while there are many shared interaction patterns and popular techniques, you'll find that each application manages its particular content object in the most relevant way for whatever it is the user is doing.

From these examples we begin to see that the highly abstracted nature of the OS layer does not extend into the application experience. Apps can be, and in many cases are, highly metaphorical experiences. Generally, smaller-scale devices are less suitable for visually complex metaphorical UIs. Small screens present many challenges to engaging users at that level, and as I explained earlier, mobile devices tend to bias towards utility. However, that is not to say a successful, highly metaphorical interface is impossible. There are many great design solutions in apps available now for the iPhone that take this approach, but we really begin to see this kind of design solution taken to its fullest effect on the iPad.

The iPad, representing a new product category, does not have the historical legacy of hyper-utility. Its focus is centered on the leisure use-case. Speed and efficiency have taken a back seat to engagement and entertainment. And while the iPad and the iPhone share the same fundamental OS, the presentation aspects of their applications diverge significantly. Obviously, display scale is the main platform characteristic driving divergence, but one of the distinct qualities that have emerged with many iPad apps is a very rich, metaphorical approach that in many cases borders on simulation. Not only is there a literal representation of an object with a high degree of visual fidelity, but the objects also react to input with a high degree of physical fidelity. While this has been possible in other computing environments before the iPad, the tangible aspect of these devices have imparted a new dimension of realism that makes this kind of approach desirable.

Metaphor and utility are only two considerations when conceptualizing your application, but be aware that they are not exclusive of one another. Take a look at the applications that you value today. How are they structured and what concepts do they employ? Do they appear to be biased more toward utility than metaphor, or is it the other way around? These questions will help you understand the value of the two approaches so you can begin to formulate your own ideas about what you believe is right for your users.

Direct Manipulation

Direct manipulation is an absolutely fundamental concept for any touch-driven UI. The basic concept is this: You directly touch the objects that you wish to interact with. Whereas with indirect manipulation you are dependent on an input device to indirectly navigate a cursor, or by other means to direct focus to an object with which you want to interact. But this is about more than fingers or mice. The key to direct manipulation is the notion that the result of your interaction with an object is so closely associated with your input that you perceive no barrier between the virtual and the real. This understanding is very important to the iOS experience. Many interactions that you may find exciting or novel on iOS devices are entirely dependent on this idea.

Users inherently understand the concept of direct manipulation because it is a reflection of how they interact with the physical world. You drag things to move them around and buttons appear to be depressed when touched. There is no hardware control set to learn, or complex set of commands to learn. Objects tend to behave in a predictable manner consistent with what you know about your world.

There are some challenges with direct manipulation. With devices like the iPhone and iPad, screen real estate is always at a premium. There is a tendency to optimize that space by creating touch controls that are small, and in some cases too small to be easily usable. Size can be a significant challenge to usability on touch screens when direct manipulation is a fundamental principle. The smaller the touch target, the more difficult it is access and operate. Small touch targets in close proximity dramatically increase the possibility of user error by providing the opportunity for mistaken input. Small targets can be difficult to identify when obscured by fingers. This can also have the effect of negating any visual feedback that may be important to a particular interaction.

We can see all of these challenges arise on the iPhone, which is a relatively extreme environment in which to attempt a robust touch-based OS. Many iPhone touch-based controls push or even exceed the boundaries of the effective ergonomics. The best example of this is the iPhone keyboard in all its variations. Apple was challenged to create a fully operational keyboard in a very limited amount of space, especially in the vertical orientation when horizontal screen width is at its minimum. The keys are too small, they are too close together, and you can't see what key that you have touched. So why does this keyboard work so well? Apple integrated a number of different techniques to mitigate the inherent ergonomic and usability issues and make this design successful. Here's what they did:

- **Target too small:** Provide visual feedback of the touched key that extends beyond the contact point of the finger.

- **Targets in close proximity:** Provide a predictive text algorithm that suggests an intended word, even if it wasn't what was typed.

- **Targets in close proximity:** Provide an inline spell-check algorithm for additional user control and refinement of input.

This represents a very robust interaction design solution and complex technical solution for one of the most problematic aspects of direct manipulation and touch screens in general: tiny buttons, squeezed together in a very small space. It's a very dangerous proposition, and unless you have the resources to create the workaround solutions to augment the core interactions and make it successful, then avoid this situation.

The reason I raise this issue within the context of direct manipulation is because scale and proximity are only really problematic when direct manipulation is the driving principle. Remember, you have to interact directly with an object in order to affect the state or condition of that object. The object is the target. But there are possible design solutions where you don't have to interact directly with an object in order to affect its condition. There may be a scenario in which a very tiny button is desirable (for whatever reason), maybe so tiny that by its appearance it is somewhat problematic. You could create a control whereby the graphic that represents it is far exceeded in scale by a "target region" that encompasses it. A user could affect that control by interacting with the target region without necessarily making contact with the actual graphical representation at the center of that target region. You can even take that concept a step further by creating situations where a target region is disassociated from its representational graphic. This is a good point from which to segue into the next topic!

Gestures

The term "gesture" is in wide use today, and depending on the context it can have very different interpretations. Sometimes the definition can be literal, as when thinking about devices that use complex machine vision to interpret the physical motion of your body as input into the computing system. When Apple refers to gestures they are specifically referencing touch interactions that allow Apple to expand their palette of input events beyond the basic input that direct manipulation might allow. In some cases this involves the simultaneous compounding of touch events (multi-touch) to invoke a particular response. But there are also examples of gestures that reside strictly in the realm of direct manipulation. At an abstract level, many gestures are the same, or at least only differentiated by subtleties of input or context of use.

The most common gestures in iOS are as follows:

- **Tap:** This is the most basic selection behavior in the OS.

- **Drag:** During a persistent touch event, an object tracks with your finger until you remove your finger from the screen.

- **Flick:** Very similar to the drag gesture, but done with greater speed. The key to this gesture is really the behavior inherent to the object itself. On release, "flickable" objects tend to display and model inertial characteristics that make the flick action relevant.

- **Swipe:** A linear brush with a finger, no direct manipulation implied, often used to reveal a hidden control.

- **Double Tap:** Two taps in short succession to designate the point of origin for image or content scaling—often a predetermined scale factor.

- **Open Pinch:** User defined up-scaling determined by how much you "open" your pinch.

- **Close Pinch:** User defined down-scaling determined by how much you "close" your pinch.

- **Long Touch:** Usually associated with invoking some form of secondary control, as with editable text to invoke the magnified view, but many other uses are possible.

There are also some newer gestures on the horizon for iOS. It will be interesting to see how quickly these are adopted and how other app developers begin to employ them. Most of these newer gestures are natural extensions of what I have listed above, and pertain more to OS level navigation and control. By that I mean they are concerned with movement through the OS, and not necessarily relevant to individual component control within a running application. The OS-level focus seems to be achieved by true multi-finger interaction (more than two fingers) to separate them from the classic set of gestures used to control applications.

Application designers and developers can do a lot with standard gesture input to add value and excitement to their products. But many gestures can be used in nonstandard ways that can still be usable, but with more compelling results. This will be covered in depth when I discuss the development of novel concepts later in this book.

The Invisible Button

The Home button, once a controversial control, is now so widely adopted and so frequently used that it is almost invisible. In previous releases of iOS, the Home button could be customized to some extent. A double click of the Home button could be configured to access the home screen, the search UI, "phone favorites," the camera, and the iPod app. Subsequent releases eliminated this functionality and have focused the Home button on the more utilitarian aspects of navigating the OS.

To understand the rethinking of the Home button for being more focused on navigation we need to look at the changing nature of iPhone usage. One of the primary drivers for the evolution of iOS has been the need to support the ever-increasing quantity of apps that users are loading onto their devices. We are seeing devices come to market with greater storage capacities designed to meet this same user demand, and this demand is in turn driven by the success of the App Store and the highly specialized nature of the apps themselves. Apple may have expected people to download a lot of apps, but they were not prepared for the very high average quantity of applications most users have. A high quantity of anything often suggests the need for an efficient means to organize as well as an efficient means to navigate that organization.

Finding an app and putting it to work was once a fairly simple proposition. All you had to do was quickly scan an array of virtual buttons on the screen.

You may have had a second screen of apps that you could quickly flick over to, but with a few simple gestures you could usually find what you sought. Fast-forward a few years and instead of having one or two screens of apps, you now have five! The relatively simple behavior of flicking back and forth between a couple of screens has now become problematic. As you move between anything more than three screens, orientation starts to become very challenging. The quick flick behavior that once made everything so easy now becomes a source of confusion as screen after screen of app icons moves past you in a rapid blur. Are you at the home screen, or are you four pages in? It can get very frustrating very quickly.

As iOS progressed, Apple designers created a number of great solutions to assist users with the challenge presented by a large number of installed apps. We can now group apps into a second-level hierarchy of user-definable app collections. We have access to an "App Switcher" that prioritizes apps by most recent use, and we can navigate directly to application via search results. We can also quickly reorient ourselves back to the home screen.

That brings us back to understanding the evolving nature of the Home button. With the increased level of functionality associated with navigation and orientation, the significance of the Home button really begins to grow. The simplistic nature of the OS-layer UI, home screen and beyond, does not allow for the addition of a navigation control set. This is very different from application-layer UI which (via the HIG) demands explicit consideration for these types of controls and a consistent model for designers and developers to follow. Without GUI components to prompt the user, ancillary navigation and orientation controls must be managed by the Home button. Within the context of the unlocked device the Home button manages the following functions:

- ▓ **Return to Home Screen:** This is the fundamental function of the Home button, and the aspect of the Home button that receives the most use.

- ▓ **Go to Spotlight:** Once the user is at the home screen, a single click takes the user to the Spotlight UI.

- ▓ **Reveal App Switcher:** The App Switcher can be revealed at any point in the OS layer or application layer.

The first two actions can be accomplished with the use of the flick gesture, but the use of the Home button makes those interactions much more efficient.

The App Switcher is different in that it is dependent on the Home button for its operation.

I think this clearly shows a pattern for how the Home button is evolving as a control dedicated to support navigation behavior. There are a few exceptions to this model, but those exceptions follow a clear pattern as well. Waking a device from its dormant mode or invoking iPod controls from the locked screen occur outside of the context of the core UI. Navigation is not a relevant function at that point in your interaction with the device, so the Home button might as well be put to good use. With that said, Apple has provided some pretty decent solutions to some of the most common use cases associated with the iPhone. Access to the iPod controls from the locked state via a double-click on the Home button is one example, another would be the ability to access Voice Control with a single long press (3 seconds). So it appears that locked-state interactions for critical use-cases is a valid use for this control too. One last exception to navigation support is the ability to configure accessibility options for the Home button that can be invoked with a triple-click.

Future releases of iOS may provide additional uses for the Home button, but that remains to be seen. We may even see the Home button eventually disappear. There are some interesting scenarios that might enable this. We may see the introduction of off-screen capacitive controls that may act as a replacement for the Home button, or we may even see new gestures emerge to control the functionality currently associated with the Home button. Rest assured, Apple will continue to evolve this aspect of their devices.

The Strange Topology of iOS

Later in this book I will delve into methods and techniques used to create interesting and unique interaction models that can be applied to iOS device apps. Before we reach that point it's worth taking some time to deconstruct some aspects of iOS that really haven't been clearly codified, or at least documented in way that helps us understand why iOS is so easily adopted by users. At the root of the iOS interaction model is a notion of a "space" through which users move fluidly to accomplish tasks. We can think about this space as a tiny little universe that the OS functionality and applications all inhabit. Like any universe, it has certain rules, limitations, and attributes that inherently affect the things that populate it. When we understand those basic mechanics we can design solutions that either use those mechanics more efficiently, or sidestep them entirely and begin to define our own rules.

iOS is essentially a planar environment, with a few exceptions. When I say "planar environment," what I mean is that the presentation of user experience at the core is a two-dimensional proposition. You may think that this is an obvious statement, since we view a screen on the device, and by their very nature the things presented on the screen are two-dimensional. That is true, but what I refer to is how interface elements are presented and how a user moves conceptually through the space inhabited by those elements. This two-dimensionality is important to recognize because we are no longer technically constrained to create user experiences that are limited to two dimensions. iPhones and iPads can render very sophisticated graphics and a volumetric UI is entirely possible, so Apple has made a conscious decision not to go in this direction (literally).

While the UI is planar, it's not strictly two-dimensional in its operation. iOS really operates between three dependent or coexistent planes. You can think of iOS as three layers of user interface, where each layer is reserved for a specific type of interaction. The movement between those layers is defined by specific set of interaction mechanics particular to the layer.

The three layers or planes of user interface break down like this, by order of importance of operation (see Figure 2-1):

- **Default Plane:** This layer is inhabited by app icons and the icon dock, and is the plane of interaction that receives the most activity from users.

- **Underlying Plane:** This is reserved for the App Switcher and for displaying contents. This space is purely a supplemental construct that supports organization, orientation, and navigation.

- **Superimposed Plane:** This layer used for dialog boxes, alerts, modal controls, and pop-overs.

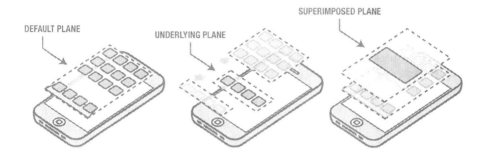

Figure 2-1. The three planes of user interface.

These planes all coexist in a very shallow visual space. From an appearance perspective these planes all lie within a few millimeters of each other. While this is simply a matter of how the graphics are rendered, the visual presentation of these planes connotes a close relationship between these spaces. It's as if the appearance of proximity supplements the cognitive association these features initially required to gain acceptance by the users. The idea of an underlying plane asserts the illusion that there was always more to this UI, literally below the surface!

The default plane of the core UI elements naturally receives the most frequent use, and by definition supports the greatest degree of interaction activity. In contrast to that, the other two planes are very limited in their interactions because they only support a limited amount of functionality. The underlying plane exists solely as a support mechanism for organization and navigation. This plane gives Apple the degree of UI scalability needed to resolve the emerging app management issues that I reviewed earlier. The underlying plane is revealed as a state change of the default plane, so those two aspects of the interaction model more accurately constitute what I would refer to as the core UI in iOS.

The superimposed plane contains objects that are very different from the app icons that populate the other two planes. There are a few ways to think about these objects; they are deliberately disruptive, they are temporary, and they do not have a "home" within the core UI. I am referring to objects such as alerts, dialog boxes, and modal controls of various types. Again, I think we take the iOS interaction model for granted, because interaction on the superimposed plane feels so natural to us. However, each of those objects could have been accounted for in the core UI in a lot of different ways. They could have reserved a portion of screen real estate to manage, but Apple determined that presenting these objects in a higher-level plane was a superior solution. Why was that? Obviously, alerts and dialogs are critical points of interaction in any kind of user interface, and bubbling those objects up and superimposing them above all other elements is a standard approach. Dialog boxes are inherently modal in nature, so they would need to disrupt activities in the core UI. Apple leverages the design pattern of the dialog for the alert, and that fact helps reinforce the understanding of how these objects operate and what users need to do when they appear. UI objects in superposition receive the least amount of interaction, but due to their nature they do receive the greatest amount of attention when they are on screen.

There is one major exception to the established spatial model. When using the iPod functions, a user has access to the classic carousel browse mode when viewing certain types of lists. The carousel view is invoked when a user rotates the device horizontally while viewing a list of songs, albums, or other media objects. The carousel view reverts to a traditional list when the device is rotated back to a vertical orientation.

The carousel view's spatial model is very different from anything I have reviewed so far. It presents objects in what appears to be a three-dimensional space. The interaction within that space is limited to the movement of objects on only one axis within a fixed frame of the horizontal view (see Figure 2-2). The notion of a fixed frame of reference is very different from the model that is in use at the top levels of the OS. The perception at that level is that a user is going from point A to point B while browsing the screens of apps. It is the perceived movement that establishes (and even defines) the concept of space. When interacting with the carousel, the user's view does not move! The user moves objects through a fixed point of view, and that fixed point of view remains unchanged no matter how many objects populate that particular frame. This is essentially an inversion of the kind of visual interaction that the user experiences with the OS as a whole.

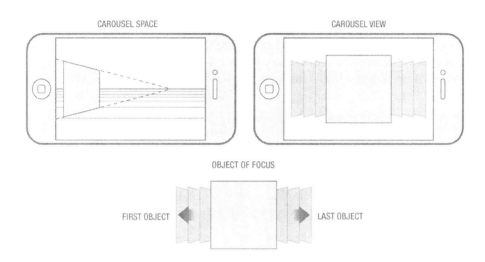

Figure 2-2. The carousel view spatial model.

Now that we have reviewed the basic visual construct of the three planes of OS interaction, we can now get into a more detailed review of how a user moves through that space. The first thing we need to establish is that those three main planes of interaction are ordered on the z axis, but the user is not required to make an explicit choice to navigate between those planes. Those three layers are really just an aspect of state pertaining to the view of the UI with which they are currently engaged, and are revealed only as needed. The dynamics of iOS spatial model are really defined by the navigation and browsing behaviors essential to device operation.

There are two basic types of movement that we can analyze: movement on the x axis and movement on the y axis. Within iOS, these two types of movements reflect very different types of interaction behavior. Movement on the x axis is most closely associated with navigation and movement on the y axis is associated with content consumption. X axis refers to right/left directionality, and when you think about it, almost all navigation happens with motion to the left or right. Browsing apps from the home screen requires a swipe to the left to bring the next screen of apps into view. A swipe to the right brings you to the search screen. The OS, at the top level, can be described as being composed of a limited set of discrete screens that extends one screen to the left, and 11 screens to the right. A user moves to the left or right through what are perceived of as discrete adjacent spaces—each adjacent space being defined by the fixed array of icons that populate it.

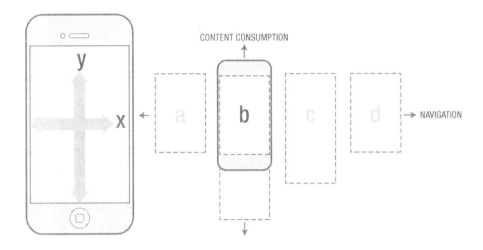

Figure 2-3. Movement & interaction behavior.

The x axis is also associated with hierarchical movement through the OS. Let's use Settings as an example to demonstrate how this works: Starting from the home screen, one swipes left till the Settings app is located. Settings is opened and you see a list of high-level options on the screen. To the right of each setting is an arrow that points to the right. Selecting a settings category, like General, initiates a transition that slides your current view to the left and off screen, while bringing the adjacent screen to right into view. You can continue to move in this fashion till you reach the bottom of the hierarchy. When going back up the hierarchy (as prompted in the upper left of the screen) the visual interaction is reversed.

The consistent use of left-right movement simplifies what would otherwise be a complex mental model for the user. Traditional approaches to hierarchical navigation often present the user with a few nonlinear methods, or shortcuts, to accelerate movement through that space. However, many of those shortcuts depend on a more comprehensive display of the hierarchical tiers, or they introduce additional points of interaction, both of which add complexity to the design solution. A device like the iPhone is limited by what it can display due to its size, so a simplified solution to hierarchical navigation is perfectly appropriate. However, I should point out that the iOS approach of one path down and the reverse path out does not hold up to deep hierarchical structures, but Apple makes it clear in the HIG that hierarchies need to be restrained for this very reason.

Movement along the y axis is not weighed down with quite as many implications as the x axis. For the most part, this type of movement is reserved for vertical scrolling behavior wherever it is required. The one observation I would call out is that there is no limitation to the length of a scrollable list. This means that virtually all y axis movement is contained within a single contiguous space. The y axis is a significant aspect of the overall spatial model and is in stark contrast to the behavior of the x axis. As I stated before, x axis movement is all about the presentation of discrete screens or deliberate chunks of space that you must move through in increments, while "y" is all about a much more fluid experience.

A significant part of what defines the spatial model is based on how we perceive the physicality of the objects, screens, controls, and other elements that populate the established space. The behavior of those items can either reinforce or undermine that model. In iOS, Apple is extremely consistent with the behavior they have imparted to all the various elements of the design. One of the most important and universal behaviors that is critical for the definition of the spatial model is their use of what I'm calling the "slide" transition. Transitions, within the context of user experience, are the visual mechanisms that denote state change to the user. Much of what we have reviewed so far in terms any perception of space has been either entirely dependent on key visual transitions or at least significantly enhanced by visual transitions. The use of transitions becomes especially useful when direct manipulation is not being employed.

Browsing applications from the home screen or sliding over to the Spotlight UI is driven directly by your touch of the screen. As your finger or thumb moves from left to right, the screen underneath tracks directly with your touch. As you explore the space and move between screens you develop an intuitive level of understanding about how that space is defined. There will always be points where direct manipulation cannot be applied, but in those situations transitions can automate visual interaction to simulate or replicate core behaviors that may be beneficial to establishing a sense of consistency for the user. iOS uses this technique in the hierarchical step navigation that I reviewed for settings. When a user has more than one choice available, it's not applicable to slide the screen to the left or right to get to another level. Instead, Apple lets you select an option, then automates a transition that is identical to the same sliding visual interaction when directly manipulating the screen.

Everything that I have reviewed so far pertains almost exclusively to the core UI of iOS. The spatial model for applications is another story altogether. Generally speaking, applications that run on top of the OS are unrestricted in terms of interaction model and design execution. The HIG certainly suggests some best practices, but that doesn't mean that you are required to follow those best practices. This means that applications may or may not replicate or mirror the spatial model inherent to the core UI of the OS, and to be sure, many applications have set out explicitly to do their own thing. Knowing that there is huge variety of apps out there, there are still some generalized behaviors that we can observe. The easiest place to identify this is on what I call the entry and exit points of the application experience, since this is common to all applications. Opening an app can happen from a few different points in the OS, and for each point there are different spatial implications:

- **From the home screen and its subsequent pages:** By far the most likely point from which a user may launch an application, the visual transition associated with this event portrays an app emerging from behind the icon array and pushing those objects away. The illusion is that the app is moving into the same plane that the icons had previously populated.

- **From the Spotlight interface:** I expect that this is likely the least used entry point of the three for the typical iOS user. In this case the Spotlight interface recedes to a point in space first, quickly followed by the selected app moving forward in space from the same vanishing point.

▪ **From the App Switcher:** App switching has its own unique behavior. Once an app is selected in the switcher, the entire active view (including the switcher) rotates out of view on the z axis, quickly followed by the desired app. All rotation appears to share the same anchor point when apps exit and enter the screen. There are few connotations of this unique visual behavior: first, it supports the idea of switching (as in toggling between two states), and second, the idea of multitasking, since the exiting app seems to be rotating just out of view—and not vanishing into oblivion.

The app exit action, as initiated by the Home button, is always the same. An app recedes back to the vanishing point from which it emerged. There isn't a direct path to Spotlight from an open app, so that scenario does not apply. Exit via app switching happens as I described it above.

What's the common theme through each of these different interactions? They all tend to stand apart from the planar presentation of the core UI and linear arrangement of space that is suggested when navigating that space. From a user's perspective, this helps establish the expectation that what they are about to embark on, from a functional perspective, is an entirely separate experience from the core UI...and in a sense that all bets are off!

I know that all of this seems obvious, but it's important to analyze and understand all of the subtle factors comprising the iOS user experience and why it is fundamentally intuitive to use. Mapping out and understanding the spatial model, at least how I have described it, gives you insight into a significant aspect of the user experience.

The Easy and the Obvious

A proper deconstruction of the iOS user experience requires me to examine and attempt to translate the philosophical underpinnings that have driven many of the important design decisions throughout the experience. Apple has done a great job of defining many of these ideas within the HIG, but it's worth taking a look at where and how they've been applied, and where and how they may have been ignored. As with any kind of guidance, there are always going to be notable exceptions that need to be reviewed.

When reading through the HIG, some patterns and themes come through loud and clear. One of the major themes is simplicity. Again, this may seem obvious, but understanding how various topics are unified and work together toward single goal tells you a lot about iOS.

Simplicity, as concept, appears to be straightforward and easily achievable—by definition. But the reality of designing complex interactive systems with simplicity in mind is another thing altogether. To compound this, the perception of simplicity does not equate to simplicity itself. What I mean is that what sometimes appears to be simple is really the result of many complex or sophisticated techniques that aren't readily apparent to the person interacting with the system. I'll try to deconstruct that gestalt quality of simplicity in iOS in terms of a few key directives identified within the HIG.

I've identified many constituent topics of this theme, but I'm certain that more could be found as well. To be clear, many of these aren't explicitly outlined in the HIG. What I've done is abstracted some key statements made in the HIG to their core so that you can understand the application of these concepts in terms of the application you are designing and/or building.

- **Finite Navigation:** Providing users with redundant means of navigation, or enhanced nonlinear navigation, is unnecessary at best, and at worst can be confusing or distracting. The ease of interaction with the device allows you to focus on creating a single clear path through your content or functionality.

- **Constrained Control Mapping:** It's more effective to identify and isolate the limited regions of your application to contain user interface elements. The controls themselves (buttons, etc.) should be perceived as secondary elements, especially in situations when application content needs to have the most prominence.

- **Constrained Control Quantity:** Limit or reduce the number of controls that you present to the user at any given point in time. To manage complex applications, distribute functions across screens and seek to group like tasks together.

- **Control Clarity:** Limit the number of unique control types when possible to avoid confusing the user. This applies not only to control type, but also to control rendering. Control functions should be identifiable by short labels and/or easily understood icons.

- **OS Offloading:** In certain situations, functionality can be removed from an application and managed at the OS level. Application settings can migrate to the iOS settings screen, helping reduce potential UI complexity.

- **User Interface Suppression:** Control elements do not necessarily need to be omnipresent. A simple gesture or touch event can invoke a control set as it is needed in the interface. The key is to provide the user with a mechanism that suggests the temporal nature of these controls and how to re-invoke them once they leave the screen.

- **Progressive Disclosure:** Strive to provide functionality only where and when it is needed within the flow of an application. It's very likely that not every feature needs to be universally available, so use that to your advantage to reduce the complexity of your screens.

- **Brand and Identity De-emphasis:** It's not necessary to hit users over the head over and over again with your brand. Identify the key points in your application where a significant brand and identity statement makes the most sense, and tone it down to an acceptable volume everywhere else.

- **State Persistence and Restoration:** Expect users to frequently engage with your application, but know that that engagement will be fractured. Mobile users are chronically multitasking, and may open and close your application many times while moving through your workflow to complete a task. Thus, you need to ensure that the state of your app is maintained as users leave it, and that the task can easily be resumed when the app is restarted.

- **Implicit Saving:** As with the issue of state persistence, any content creation tasks must be preserved and the notion of "saved" should be implicit to any workflow.

- **Gestural Restraint:** Limit the number of unique gestures required to interact with your application. Understanding gesture usage or having to learn new gestures can be a significant barrier to the adoption of your application.

- **Hierarchical Restraint:** Restraint of hierarchical depth is really an aspect of the successful implementation of finite navigation. A high degree of hierarchical structure makes it difficult to design a simple and easily understood path through an application. That doesn't mean that it is impossible, it just means that you will be challenged with managing user orientation or challenged with trying to eliminate the tedium of moving through that hierarchy.

- **App Modality:** A user can really only view and interact with one application at time. The App Switcher suggests that there may be multiple apps running concurrently, but even in that case a user is required to toggle between apps to do anything. At this point there is no such thing as simultaneous app viewing, but that may be a possibility in the future with larger format devices like the iPod.

All of these topics point toward the theme or directive of simplicity, and in doing so cross over or complement one another considerably. However, there are also various topics that seem to contradict this direction too. These ideas are sprinkled throughout the HIG and have interesting implications for how you may think about your application.

The first few issues I want to raise pertain to the topics reviewed in this section. I first want to call out that while the concept of UI suppression can be used to manage screen complexity, it potentially shifts a greater cognitive load over to the user. When the UI elements are not on screen, the user is required understand where they went, how they got there, and what they need to do to bring them back. This isn't necessarily a problem when managed in a simple and direct way, but if this requires any kind of complex interaction it can lead to significant problems for the user.

I'd also like to point out that universal labeling of controls can become problematic in cases where you are unable to limit control quantity on screen. Labels require room, and sometimes there is just not enough room for a legible label. And there are cases that even when there may be room to account for a label, the presence of labels can increase the perceived complexity of the elements on screen.

Another interesting point within the HIG is an emphasis on high information density and high functional density for applications. This seems to fly in face almost every topic that I reviewed before. The HIG states that app authors should

> *...strive to provide as much information or functionality as possible for each piece of information people give you. That way, people feel they are making progress and are not being delayed as they move through your application.*

At face value this seems contradictory, but I think Apple is trying to make the point that you should provide the user with a high degree of interaction efficiency to avoid frustration.

Summary

In this chapter I covered a number of topics intended to deconstruct many of the subtleties of the iOS user experience. From the overview you can see how many discrete ideas and techniques are utilized in concert to really engage the user in a way that actively manages their perceptions.

The iOS bias toward a more utilitarian approach appears to be a rational evolution from the smartphone legacy of days gone by, but this may increasingly be limited to the domain of smaller-scale devices like the iPhone. As the iPad and other medium-format devices come into their own, legacy concerns around utility and efficiency will become less relevant.

The idea of direct manipulation is the foundation for all touch interactions. Users are presented with a model where the result of interaction with an object is so closely associated with their input or action that no barrier is perceived between the virtual and the real.

Gestures evolve the capabilities of touch interfaces beyond the baseline interactions accounted for with direct manipulation.

The Home button is the only hardware input to directly control the core UI of iOS. It's important to recognize the limits of its operation and how that folds into the interaction model of iOS as a whole. The role it plays in supporting navigation and orientation as its primary function has remained its focus as the OS evolves.

iOS presents the user with an easily understood spatial model, and this is a significant factor contributing to the perception of ease of use. The spatial model is established by the consistent use of visual interactions and passive transitions that allow users to navigate in a predictable manner.

A philosophical imperative to keep things simple drives many of the design decisions that have made iOS easy to use and understand. This philosophy can be identified at various points in the HIG that at first glance may seem to be unrelated. However, all of these points work in concert to help manage functional complexity and interaction complexity.

User Experience Differentiation and Strategy

The first two chapters of this book were dedicated almost entirely to understanding the nature of iOS at a detailed level. Knowing the rationale for a
particular interaction is just as important as understanding its mechanics. The
review of the HIG and the deconstruction of the mechanics of iOS give you a
solid, baseline understanding of the type of experience that Apple wants to
deliver to their users. The mere existence of the HIG tells us that Apple places a high priority on raising the level of execution for iOS applications, with
the intention that third-party developers will meet the high expectations of
Apple's users.

We know what Apple wants you to do and we know why they want it that
way. But are there situations where it makes sense to diverge from the HIG?
How do you know how far to push your design solution? One of the purposes
of this book is to provide you with the tools and guidance to help make those

decisions, stand out in a crowd, and get that "WOW" reaction critical to the success of your application.

Being different for the sake of being different may be enough to get you started, and it may take you down a path to creating an amazing app. However, that may not be enough for everyone to get started and certainly it may not be enough to justify your design decisions if you ultimately answer to a chief financial officer or to investors. A simple thought experiment will begin to help you make your case. Let's assume that you are interested in creating a new application for an iPad or iPhone. Do you say to yourself, "Hey, I've got a great idea for an app! And it's going to be just like the competition!"? Of course not. When you look at it that way you can see that being different should be a critical aspect of your business model, marketing plan, and user experience strategy.

Shifting Perceptions and Expectations

Outside of potential business models, marketing plans, and other "go to market" strategies, it is important to recognize that you are about to enter a highly competitive environment where just getting noticed is a significant achievement. Even when your app is noticed, users quickly and happily move on to the next great thing when it becomes available. This situation has been exacerbated by the evolution of user expectations around their interaction with technology in general.

Over the past few years we've seen the rapid adoption of radically new interaction behaviors. We tend to take this for granted because these behaviors have quickly become mainstream. The iPhone and iPad are excellent examples of this. Before those devices came to market, capacitive touchscreen interface technology was not something that the general public understood or desired. Without any demand, there really wasn't any push to integrate that technology into products beyond a few experimental instances or poorly executed commercial products. Then the iPhone came to market and demonstrated the power of that technology when combined with simple and straightforward interaction. The initial impact of those multitouch interactions generated quite a splash in the consciousness of the consumer. Now, over 4 years later we are in a situation were that technology and its associated interactions are considered de rigueur.

Another classic example is the Nintendo Wii and its associated game controller, often called the WiiMote. The integration of accelerometers into the control mechanism combined with other sensing technologies enabled Nintendo to create an entirely new category of gameplay. Even though the interactions enabled by the WiiMote were radically different from anything that had preceded it, people flocked to stores to buy the new console and it soon outsold everything else on the market. Competitors like Sony and Microsoft were forced to quickly develop similar technologies to address the shift in consumer expectations around console gameplay.

These examples demonstrate a significant shift in mass-market expectations about how people can interact with technology—all of which is being driven by the emergence of various types of enabling technologies such as accelerometers and capacitive touch screens. Some of these technologies have significant implications for the design and specification of interaction on their own, but there are also scenarios where more mundane technologies have been combined to synthesize new types of experiences as well. The shift that I describe is a kind of cultural critical mass emerging around the expectation and acceptance of the "different." The consumer expects that products will have some new kind of new, compelling interaction that they've never seen before, and in many cases this factor is helping drive purchasing decisions.

The market for digital products (consumer electronics, software, etc.) is seeing a rapid co-evolution of *experience*—that which we design and create, and *those who experience*—the users or consumers of the products we are designing. This is essentially a feedback loop. As more compelling or unique interactions are introduced to the market (as associated with various product releases), we see greater demand and increased acceptance for increasingly unique and compelling interaction. I would expect that at some point we would begin to see this trend level off, but since contemporary society is a consumer-driven culture we can expect this feedback loop to continue for some time. The bottom line is that new interaction behaviors and techniques are expected, and these factors are critical to achieving any level of market differentiation.

Usability and Adoption

The environment I just described presents another shift in how to view the creation of interaction design solutions. Classically, the success of any given interaction design solution has been measured by its usability. This was a very sensible approach during the era where we saw the initial introduction of digital technologies to mass-market consumers. Transitioning consumers from well-established and culturally entrenched analog behavior in the real world, to its counterpart in a highly abstract computational environment, was a huge challenge. Looking back to the 20-year span from the early 1980s to the early 2000s, the amount of technological change in the consumer space has been phenomenal. Technological progress in that period was mirrored by the increasing quality of user experience, which at that point was almost always expressed in terms of usability.

"Usability" at that time was an engineering mindset, and the usability of a system was established by quantitative means through a number of different product design and development techniques. This was all well and good, but as the market for digital products began to explode at the turn of the century, it became necessary to explore other means by which one could compete in the market. This led to the emergence of the more comprehensive "user experience" mindset and its gestalt approach to product design. That mindset included usability, but also encompassed aesthetics, perception, and emotional engagement on the part of the user.

An Argument For Desire

Now that the user experience mindset is well-established, the emphasis on usability has changed somewhat. It hasn't gone away at all, nor should it, but it really needs to be approached as a basic consideration. You must assume that all of your competitors will come to market with a fundamentally usable product, so you need to make a determination about the other factors of user experience that will make your product more desirable. This begins to touch on the main points for this chapter; that the benchmark for success is really more about the adoption of a design solution (in this case an application). Usability plays a significant role in driving adoption, but desire in many respects is much more important. Effectively solving for desire means being cognizant of all the factors I have described so far:

- Understanding the evolving state of users, including their expectations and perceptions of contemporary interaction

- Understanding how the user experience of your product can be different from that provided by your competitors

- Understanding that you may need to focus on engendering desire if adoption is your priority

- Engendering desire, given the environment we design for today, may require the exploration of unorthodox solutions

User Experience Strategy

Understanding the context for your user experience decisions is very important, but it's really only a starting point on your way to a more comprehensive strategy. A good user experience strategy is all about establishing a clear vision and plan for your organization. Providing an understanding or definition for an approach to user experience is more important than addressing specific design details at this point. A good strategy should provide a substantial framework that will help guide your decisions as you progress through the design process. It's not so much about the *what*, as it is about the *how*. Knowing that technologies, user needs, and user desires will be in a constant state of flux, it's important to have a clear plan about how that state of flux be resolved. Tactical details are an aspect of execution as it has been defined in your strategy.

Putting an effective strategy in place has a number of benefits:

- It will provide an excellent point of unification for the diverse teams involved in the development of the product.

- It will ensure customer satisfaction by helping teams maintain intense focus on the user.

- It provides a consistent experience through the lifecycle of your product, maintaining established user expectations or helping evolve those expectations when necessary.

- It will almost certainly improve the quality of your product and help mitigate any deployment risks.

These are all particularly important points when trying to achieve a high degree of impact or "Wow" with a unique design solution for your app. High-impact user experiences are very likely to present a number of engineering and design challenges that will have to be managed in a highly coordinated way. Having a shared vision around the solution is critical, and a well-crafted strategy should provide this. Your strategy becomes even more important if a product portfolio expands and needs to evolve over time.

Defining Your Strategy

What exactly does a user experience strategy entail? At the highest level it is about establishing a set of perceptual goals targeted at a specific group(s) of users and understanding how those goals can be addressed by different aspects of the application experience. Those goals may address a particular feature set relevant to how users may perceive the value or usefulness of an app. They may pertain to a series of critical use-cases from a purely functional perspective, or they may address how features support or reflect the user's lifestyle.

All of this is highly dependent on the nature of the application, but in all cases a strategy should define how those features are presented to the user in a way that speaks to the stated goals.

There are other dimensions of complexity that should not be overlooked. A good strategy should address the maturation of user experience over time through the periodic reevaluation of goals, users, and market conditions. If the development team is operating under an Agile methodology, then it may be easier to integrate this kind of design thinking into the overall process and integrate revisions to user experience by way of a product backlog. This approach would be the type of thing that would be documented in the user experience strategy.

No user experience stands alone anymore. Thinking about user experience as being isolated to just your application can get you into a lot of trouble. In many cases user experience needs to be accounted for across many touch points in a larger continuum. This would be true for large, complex product families where systematic user experience dependencies need to be tracked or managed. Even applications that stand alone need to be understood from an end-to-end experience. Be sensitive to all aspects of your users' journey; from the discovery of your application via search engine, App Store, or product page, through the install and update process, even to how you may ultimately sunset your product.

It's also worth taking a look at the larger ecosystem that may ultimately be responsible for the distribution of your app. For the purposes of this book, that would be Apple's App Store in its various incarnations. You don't have control over the App Store workflow, but you do control the content on your product page and other small but highly relevant details. Do your best to leverage the aspects of the App Store that Apple lets you control. Always look for opportunities to use those capabilities to your advantage by seeking to reinforce your user experience strategy. There are limited opportunities to do this, but a first step is how you approach your app icon, and how that relates to the elements you select to be displayed on screen. Establishing some baseline criteria for the screens you want to display and making sure those criteria align with or support your strategy is also very important. Even the tone andw voice of your text description can play a role in reinforcing your overall user experience strategy.

This is a lot to account for, and you may not get it all right on the first try, but ultimately your strategy will pay off as users start to engage with your product and move through each of those touch points.

Thinking Through Differentiation

Product differentiation can be a significant factor in achieving a high degree of impact, or "Wow." We've covered the rationale for this kind of thinking, but there are many nuances that need to be understood before beginning any design activities. A good user experience strategy needs to outline these nuances in a clear and coherent way.

The first thing that needs to be understood is that differentiation can be viewed along a continuum. The nature of that continuum is up to you, but you should approach differentiation as a range of possible options between two opposing points. One approach would be to think about one point being *similar* and the other *divergent* (see Figure 3-1). Similar and divergent are just abstract ideas to give you a framework for thinking about where your design solution needs to reside. In this case, similar speaks to a more traditional approach, one that has its basis in conventional wisdom. It represents a lowrisk, follower mentality. At the other end of the scale, divergent refers to an unorthodox approach that may be higher-risk, but demonstrates innovation. The actual scale depends on what your strategy states as the desired goals for your product. The question is, where on that scale does your app need to be positioned to be competitive or desirable, assuming those are goals? Your application's position on that scale can provide some indication of whether to consider an incremental enhancement of existing functionality, or a radical reinvention.

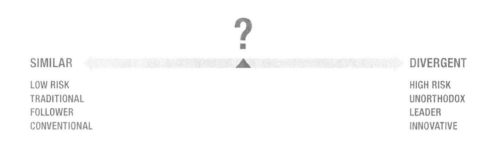

Figure 3-1. Continuum of differentiation.

You can apply this approach to any aspect of your user experience. The example that I just used could be looking at that scale in terms of functional differentiation, but you may want to apply this same method to your thinking about a potential interaction model, independent of functional concerns. If functionality is unchanged between possible options, you may want to identify that your primary differentiation is focused on interaction. You can plot where you think the interaction model needs to be on that scale and use that as another guidepost to help direct your interaction design activities.

This kind of thinking isn't limited to one dimension. Concepts can be plotted on multiple axes to converge on a specific kind of perception on the part of the user. But at the very least you can start by addressing the level of differentiation you are trying to achieve on that basic, two-dimensional continuum.

How do you go about determining the right direction for your app? The first point to consider is whether you are creating a new application or working with an existing application. A new application doesn't carry the burden of a legacy user experience and can be a blank slate for the design team. If you are working with an existing application, the nature of your release is an important factor in the decision-making process. With existing applications, try to reserve significant alterations to a user experience for major releases.

Know Your Users

The biggest factor in determining what direction to take with your application is based on what you know about your users. These could be existing users, or these could be the hypothetical users you are targeting with an entirely new app. The more you understand about your users, the more you will know about how to craft the details of your user experience strategy.

There is a huge benefit in putting together some fundamental research about the nature of your users well before you engage in developing your application. In many cases, the best way to start is to take a stab at defining a user persona. You may already have a vision about the nature of your application, and that might include some assumptions about who that app will appeal to and why it will be desirable. Use those assumptions to craft a persona about a hypothetical user. A persona should contain enough information for you and members of the design team to identify with the user at some level. Age, gender, income level, and job title are important details, but you should also include domestic and familial information to help complete the picture. Lifestyle information is also important; the more you can define interests, hobbies, and social activities, the better the persona will be. For the last piece of the puzzle, you need to include some information about their motivations and goals. A generalized statement about goals and motivation is fine, but you may want to apply those to a particular use-case. This sounds like a daunting task if you are trying to fabricate a user persona from scratch, but you can get a head start on the process if you base a persona on someone you already know. You may want to represent that person accurately, but you always have the option to embellish details and add information to make sure the persona is representative of the type of user you target.

You may feel highly confident that the persona or personas that you outlined are an accurate snapshot of the type of user(s) that you seek. If you are not confident, or if you feel that you may not have enough detail in place, then you may want to consider validating the persona at one level or another. There are a few different ways to do this. If you want to keep the process more informal, you can engage other members of the team to confirm your assumptions or contribute additional details. You also have the option to validate your user personas more formally, in which case you'll need to recruit and screen for individuals with the same basic attributes and interview them. Your line of questioning should be such that you can make a determination as to the accuracy of your assumptions around the personas. You will likely find yourself learning many additional details from these individuals that will be valuable to include in personas you have already established.

Once you have a persona in place you can use that information to model different types of scenarios related to the use of your application. Mapping a persona to a scenario allows you to role-play and experience a hypothetical application through the eyes of your target audience. To do this effectively you need to think and behave in accordance with what you have documented about a particular user. It's not as easy as it sounds, but with a good grasp of the persona you are designing for, you can understand the type of user experience that they would value. It may be important to document these scenarios in detail. Scenarios can take the form of a short written narrative, or you may visualize a scenario in a sequence of storyboards. It may also be valuable to align your scenarios with specific use-cases where specific features or feature sets are highlighted.

Evaluating Competitors

With your user personas established and scenarios in place, it's time to look outward to the market and get some insight into to what your competitors are doing. Evaluating your competition isn't difficult and since you already have a vision for what you app is going to be, you may already have a sense of your competition's strengths and weaknesses. This assumes that you know who your competition is. If you don't know, then your first step is to identify your competitors. For the purposes of this effort this includes any app that provides similar functionality. With the App Store in place, finding competitors is simple task. Just enter the appropriate search criteria and review the results for relevant applications. Depending on the nature of the app, you might have a number of competitors available in the App Store. You do not need to account for all these. You only want to benchmark the best applications, and again, the App Store store makes this very easy. Filter your search results by star rating, and find apps with excellent reviews. You'll ultimately want to narrow your set down to three to five applications.

Now that you have your competition identified, you'll want to start exploring these apps in detail. While doing so, document your observations and experiences. Even make note of how you feel as you use the various functions and execute tasks. Some apps may provide great features, while others support great interaction. No detail should go unexamined, but you may want to focus on specific issues of importance to your app. Document anything that you find to be appealing or of value. The same is true for anything that you find unappealing or poorly executed. Once you have a critical mass of observations in place, group and cluster related observations under high-level themes. These observations and themes can significantly inform your overall strategy, and you can refer to them as points of validation for or against various aspects of your app's user experience.

Leading the Market

A huge component of achieving the "Wow" is making sure that you get your app in users' hands at the right time. The perception of your app's experience can be affected by what's already in the market and popular with users. Your differentiation approach and unique interactions that you worked so hard to create can quickly become irrelevant if a competitor beats you to market with a similar user experience. The impact of your app can also be diffused if the competition releases an app shortly after yours. Avoiding these situations can be tricky, but if you plan accordingly it can be done. An effective user experience strategy needs to address the positioning of an app and the desired perceptions on the part of the user—not for the current state of the market, but for the predicted future state. I not referring to the point in time that may be planned for your app's release. I'm talking about trying to lead the market by a defined period of time with your user experience.

Getting out in front of the market requires sophistication on the part of your design team, and I'll certainly be reviewing the process by which you can get to a great design solution, but your strategy needs to outline the vision for this leadership too. No matter what the vision or goals are, you can predict if your design solutions will achieve your goals if you test against the right users. In this case, you will want to find individuals who define themselves as influencers to their peers. Influencers are not predisposed to follow trends, but more apt to establish trends. These are users who see themselves as cultural curators to their peer group. Testing concepts with these types of users gets you out in front of the adoption curve, and away from the conventional wisdom of the mass market that may be holding you back from creating the next great app. These people need to be consistent with the personas that have been defined, just screened for the various influencer characteristics.

Summary

Users and user experience technology have evolved considerably over the past 20 years. Expectations around what software should be and how it should work have shifted significantly. Users not only expect highly differentiated, innovative user interfaces, they embrace them wholeheartedly when those experiences are executed thoughtfully.

Successful interaction design solutions of the past were defined almost entirely by their usability. Usability at that time was an engineering mindset focused on improving products through quantitative user input. As the market evolved, it became necessary to look beyond usability and understand other aspects of an application experience to remain competitive. The mindset of "user experience" addresses this by taking a comprehensive view of aesthetics, perception, and emotional engagement.

Usability is now a table stakes consideration. In order to drive adoption with users you need to make a determination about other the factors of user experience that will make your application more desirable. You can't ignore usability by any means, but desire needs to be the focus of your design solution.

Having a user experience strategy in place will ensure that you make the right decisions as you progress through the design process.

- It will provide an excellent point of unification for the diverse teams involved in the development of the product.
- It will ensure customer satisfaction by helping teams maintain sharp focus on the user.
- It will provide a consistent experience through the lifecycle of your product, maintaining established user expectations.
- It will almost certainly improve the quality of your product and help mitigate any deployment risks.

You user experience strategy should include the following information:

- Well-defined user personas that include details about their motivations and goals.
- How features are determined, managed, or organized based on how the user perceives value.

- How use-cases and workflows are formulated and how they are relevant to the lifestyle attributes, motivations, and goals of a particular user.

- How to manage the maturation of user experience over time, beyond just a feature road map, but by also accounting for how the core interactions need to evolve.

- A broad view of the higher-level user experience continuum, either for the acquisition and download lifecycle and/or an applications relationship and integration with other product family members.

- Competitive insights that can guide, validate, and inform various aspects of your user experience as it is formulated.

With all these items in place, you can feel confident that your strategy will provide enough guidance and direction for how you want to shape your user experience.

The Killer App

Designing for the
Mobile Context

You may already have a well-defined application targeted for iOS devices that you'd like to build. If you've reviewed Chapter 3 you know that your application may be refined or made more robust by thinking in terms of a more comprehensive user experience strategy. As you start to think through specific use-cases and as you start to flesh out profile-based scenarios, it becomes increasingly important to get your head around the usage context for mobile devices. Armed with that knowledge you can validate and elaborate on your existing idea and really focus on the creation of a "killer app" for an iPhone or iPad.

To provide you with a solid foundation, I'm going to review the importance of the mobile space for application developers, and give you a framework for thinking about the behavioral differences between the iPad and iPhone that will help you shape those experiences in the right way for your users. I'll then walk through some guidance on targeting specific use-cases to help ensure that your application hits your user's sweet spot.

The Importance of Mobile

Okay, we all know that the mobile space is red-hot right now, and if you have picked up this book you understand the potential that mobile devices have for delivering some very interesting apps and experiences. But why is mobile so important and what is driving the enthusiasm around the mobile app space?

The core value of mobile computing in any context is the idea of anytime, anywhere access to data and functionality. It's really that simple. Over a very short time we have seen the evolution of these "phones" go from an exclusive focus on telephony, to a point where telephony is virtually a fringe use-case in what is otherwise a universal computing appliance. The success and popularity of devices like the iPhone is based on the fact that they have made computing and the digital experience much more relevant through their universal accessibility.

In the past, working with software or accessing the internet were chair-bound activities that limited you to a specific place and time. You had to be at home or at work to take advantage of applications or to browse the internet. Even while at home, the setting and mode of interaction with the computing environment was a highly formalized affair, with keyboard and mouse arranged just so in a special room or nook dedicated to the activity. Generally speaking, computer usage at home or at work was primarily task driven, with only a small portion of that time open to leisure activities. Obviously, I'm speaking in generalities here, but the point is that before now, our physical and environmental interactions with computing environments like a desktop PC were incredibly constrained.

By eliminating the limitations of place and time you can start to open up entirely new possibilities, new use-cases, and new apps to explore. This is the core value of mobile computing on devices like the iPhone: the combination of high-value computational experiences with entirely new scenarios where one is not limited to the home or office. There is an incredible opportunity to rethink how these devices, their software, and the data that feeds into them can augment various aspects of our lives—and not just limit their use to individual segments of our day. It is precisely this synthesis that is helping drive the extremely rapid growth and adoption of the iPhone and the powerful applications that it puts in the palm of your hand. It is through the understanding of this technological and cultural shift that all functional and user experience decisions should be made.

It probably worth pausing at this point to extend the conversation beyond the purely mobile mindset and set some parameters for thinking about the wider implications of iOS devices.

Mobile Experience versus Portable Experience

When talking about mobile, I'm clearly referring to the iPhone and all that it entails. However, we have another category of device that must be put into context as well, which for all practical purposes cannot be strictly referred to within the "mobile" definition that is part of our common understanding.

When Apple launched the first-generation iPad in 2010, they did so with the clear intention of creating a new category of device to reside somewhere between a laptop or netbook and a smartphone. Along with the usual hype and enthusiasm that precedes any Apple product release, there were some detractors that questioned the value of a device. From their perspective, the iPad was just a giant iPhone. What these detractors failed to recognize was that there were significant implications inherent to the larger form factor of the iPad that would align with all sorts of interesting use-cases that were just not practical for either an iPhone or laptop of any size (MacBook or otherwise).

Both the iPhone and the iPad are much more "mobile" than a typical laptop, but because of their size difference there are significantly different behaviors associated with each device. First let's recognize that mobile phones are inherently personal devices. Your phone is directly associated with you. A call to your phone is a call targeted at you, and in many ways people view your phone as a proxy for yourself. People commonly will say, "I called you...," as opposed to being more literal and saying, "I called your phone...". This starts to suggest how tightly correlated these devices are to our identities.

Our mobile phones are with us everywhere we go. They are a constant companion that never leaves our side. The biggest factor contributing to this is that fact that iPhones are small enough to make this feasible and practical. The size of the iPad negates this value. It is carried easily enough, but it's size precludes it from the type of true mobility that the iPhone enables.

The iPad's weakness is also its strength. Although the size of it makes it impractical to carry with you everywhere you go, the iPad's large screen provides a much better experience for many types of activities that one may find challenging on the iPhone's small display. Reading text, browsing the web, and watching videos are possible on an iPhone, but the large display of the iPad makes those otherwise tedious tasks a joy for the user to perform. The market continues to reinforce this bias and subsequently the iPad as emerged as the definitive "casual computing" device. The notion of casual computing is not new, but with the iPad the idea has taken on the connotation of leisure orientation and all that implies for the types of digital content and experiences available to us today.

This starts to point us to one of the key differentiators between the iPhone and the iPad. If we know that iPad usage is casual and very often leisure focused, we can infer that the period of engagement with those activities is relatively long. Watching a movie or TV show on an iPad requires some available time and uninterrupted focus. The same is true for reading your favorite newspaper or the latest bestselling novel. In contrast to that, checking your iPhone for the latest stock quotes, current weather, or the latest updates on your social network of choice are quick, short-term interactions. However, because you have this device with you everywhere you go, you can dive in to those experiences at any time, even while simultaneously engaging in other activities. As any iPhone user knows, it quickly becomes force of habit to pull out your phone and check it at every available opportunity. In that sense, usage behavior between the two devices is almost diametrically opposed. I'll restate it like this:

- **iPhone:** High frequency of use, but the engagement is short in duration.

- **iPad:** Low frequency of use, but the engagement is much longer in duration.

This isn't universally true, but as a general observation it is an accurate way to differentiate behaviors between the two devices.

The implications of these usage patterns for the idea of mobility are very interesting. We now need to make a point of distinction between how users approach these devices. I think it is fair to say that the iPhone truly represents the idea of mobility in the sense that we understand it today, but the iPad is a different thing altogether. It is not a mobile device as such; it represents a "portable" model of computing that may be different from anything that has preceded it. I say portable, in the sense that it often travels with you and it is not a burden to have it by your side, but it does not have the universal presence or level of personal affinity that your iPhone has.

The idea of portability as a nuanced subset of mobile computing is evident in the kind of scenarios we see emerging with everyday iPad use. Remember, iPad usage is lower in frequency, but when users do engage with the device they do so for quite a while. So users need to be somewhere where they are going to be stationary for a while. The home is the perfect setting for this kind of behavior. So when I talk about portability, in many cases this is just describing the movement of the device from room to room within the home. Users certainly take their iPads everywhere, but the actual behavior for usage is identical to what they would do at home: sitting, in a relaxed position with the iPad in the lap. Again, thinking about frequency of use, while the home is the place where an iPad probably sees the greatest degree of usage, the frequency of usage will drop as a user moves with the device to new locations. The logic being that outside of the home, the opportunities for casual engagement in a comfortable and stationary setting start to decrease.

The iPad presents another behavioral difference as well. Although the iPhone possesses a deep level of personal affinity, the iPad is a different situation because of the lack of fully integrated telephony. This is a considerable factor in how users perceive this device. Because it is not explicitly associated with an individual, the way a phone is, users are more apt to share the usage of this device with others. This effect is amplified when the iPad is viewed as a secondary device in situations where users may already own an iPhone, or an iPhone plus a laptop. These other two devices are more likely to be perceived as the primary devices for communication and productivity, thereby making owners more comfortable with communal iPad use. A good example of this may be the home environment. Individual family members may have their own phones or even their own laptops, but the use of the iPad is shared among the family for various purposes.

Critical Use-Cases for Mobile

There are many ways to target your application for optimal use on mobile and portable devices, but let's first start by assuming that you already have some baseline features and functionality in mind. Your consideration of platform might already account for mobile-specific use-cases based on the guidance that I have already provided, however it's also important to look at some critical use-cases at a high level to understand how your application relates, or may need to relate to them.

I have identified five major use-cases that have proven to provide value to users across many contexts and scenarios. I wouldn't go so far as to say they are universal, but I'm sure that you can identify many applications that you personally could not live without, and that you currently have on your iPhone or iPad.

I am positioning these as use-cases, but they could also be considered application categories or even thought of as feature sets. Taking the position of use-case is relevant because it suggests a user-centered bias, and that makes sense from the perspective of having an established user experience strategy as foundation for your design activities. As you will see, the notions of categories and feature sets will play a role in the overview that follows.

There are five critical use-cases that you need to be aware of when thinking about your app:

- Communication
- Entertainment
- Location-Based Services
- Commerce
- Utility

It's likely that at one level or another, these categories probably cover just about every application in existence, mobile, portable, or otherwise, but let's walk through what each of these use-cases represents for the overall mobile context.

Communication

I think it's fair to say that communication is a table-stakes use-case. Obviously, with an iPhone this is fundamental to the perceived value of the device, considering that 1:1 communication via telephony is really what drove the creation of that platform. However, communication goes much farther than just telephony and the robust features associated with the mobile platform. You need to be thinking about communication in it's broadest sense. One way to do that is to break down communication into two basic modalities. The first mode being "one-to-one" communication, and second mode being "one-to-many" communication. I'll outline the types of functionality that fall into each of those categories and you'll see why this is a use-case to always keep in the forefront of your mind.

One-to-One Communication

Each of these four modes are not exclusively one to one because there are additional functions associated with each that let you engage with more than one individual. The important thing to note is that at their core they enable a one-to-one connection.

- Basic Telephony / Voice
- Email
- SMS
- Instant Messaging

One-to-Many Communication

Let's assume that the list above can be included here, but the point of this list is to demonstrate that the definition of communication may be broader and deeper than how you are thinking about it today.

- Social networking channels (Facebook, Google+, Twitter)
- **Media sharing channels** (YouTube, Flickr, Vimeo, etc.)
- A/V Podcasts
- Blog Posts
- Comments
- Forums

You can see that when you break down the use-case into the various modes and capabilities, the value becomes very apparent. Many of the most success-ful applications address these communication modes directly, mapping their functionality directly to a mobile app, or they integrate some aspect of that functionality as a value add to their own core feature set.

Entertainment

This is a huge catchall use-case that can be interpreted in many different ways. Entertainment as a category is ambiguous enough, but at the abstract level it has to be recognized as another absolutely critical use case. The main factor here is that the dimension of entertainment is really a consideration of user perception and attitude as applied to any use-case. For example, even reviewing your financial portfolio and current stock quotes can be considered entertaining under the right conditions.

That's all well and good, but it doesn't give you much to go on in terms of modeling functions or understanding how your app may address the use-case. To give you something more concrete, let's break "entertainment" down into the two subcategories that we know have a significant role helping drive the adoption of iOS devices.

- Gaming
- Content Consumption

Mobile gaming is obviously the easiest identifiable critical use-case in the entertainment category. There is a lot of sophistication associated with how games are positioned in the mobile space, and there are many schools of thought around what kind of gameplay is most successful on the various mobile platforms. For the purposes of this book, we won't delve into the esoteric aspects of gaming interactions, though many of the ideas that I have reviewed so far are applicable to the creation of games for iOS.

Aside from gaming, you have to recognize that content consumption, in all it's various forms, is a very large component of any entertainment-oriented use-case. Watching videos, listening to music, reading books, browsing the web, and many other activities are all encapsulated within that category. Many of the most popular apps for both the iPhone and the iPad are almost exclusively focused on content consumption, each with its own value-added user experience to make that consumption more entertaining or more attractive to users. Clearly others have seen the value of this use-case and are capitalizing on it already. Even with that being the case, there is still plenty of consumer demand for more apps focused on helping users consume content in new and interesting ways.

Location-Based Services

Location-based services are a critical category in the mobile context, and really the only use-case explicitly unique to mobile. Location-based services are an emergent factor derived from the combination of many different enabling technologies available on mobile devices today. Integrated GPS, digital compass technology, and mobile network information provide an incredible level of detail and accuracy regarding the location and orientation of the user.

There are a number of applications in the App Store that integrate location-based services in interesting ways, some of which are very successful, and some that are not. For the most part this is still a very nascent use-case and app developers are only scratching the surface on what is possible with these technologies. Most applications seem to focus on either helping the user broadcast where they are (one-to-one and one-to-many communication tied to location), or they are focused on helping users go from point A to point B. The big question is: What is the inherent value of location-based services, and how should you be thinking about this use-case for the application that you have in mind? The answer is simple, location-based services and all the capability that implies are about adding relevance and meaning to the content and/or functionality.

Commerce

Commerce is another one of those critical use-cases that is just about universal to any platform. It's worth mentioning because it is something that shouldn't be ignored, and like some of the other use-cases I've reviewed, there are many ways to think about it. The first thing that probably comes to mind is the basic ecommerce model that we are intimately familiar with in the desktop/web environment. Browsing for products, reading reviews and adding items to a shopping cart is practically second nature to us all now. The challenge with straightforward commerce applications in the mobile context is understanding how platform-specific interactions need to be applied to the general workflow. Beyond that, it's about optimizing critical interactions, like product browsing, for speed, efficiency, and screen economy.

That's a relatively simplistic view of what the commerce use-case could address. There's much more potential with this use-case if you look beyond being able to support a basic transactional situation and think about commerce in a much broader sense. There are a number of "augmentation scenarios" that are just beginning to be explored. These are use-cases that seek to support or augment existing shopping behavior or other commerce activities, without the need for explicit transaction support.

I've broken these down into two main categories:

- **Curation:** Leveraging third-party sources to help navigate complex product choices to provide recommendations and influence purchasing behavior.

- **Aggregation:** Automated filtering and management of content (in this case products) from disparate sources by a set of user-defined parameters

This is just the tip of the iceberg. The definition of your user experience strategy and details associated with the personas you are designing for will help expose other interesting commerce augmentation use-cases that you may want to take advantage of.

Utility

In Chapter 2, I reviewed the general utilitarian ethos driving the design of the overall user experience. This is also a highly relevant factor in the perception of value for applications installed on the device. The idea of utility is in stark contrast to the entertainment category that I reviewed previously, and in a sense, has more weighted relevance for the true mobile use of an iPhone, rather than the portable scenario that I outlined for the iPad. Going back to our understanding of how those devices are differentiated in the mind of the user, this makes a lot of sense. Applications that can achieve a high degree of function, or utility can be very successful, despite a lack of sophisticated graphics or dynamic interactions. If an application can help a user execute a task quickly and efficiently, it will definitely see a lot of use.

The idea of utility is pretty broad, but again, in the context of mobility you can begin to frame your application in a way to address this use-case.

If this is where you are targeting your application, there are two dimensions that your application need fulfill:

- **Right Function:** Providing the right functional density from which a task may be executed.

■ **Task Efficiency:** Providing the simplest means by which a task may be executed.

If utility is the goal, then those two points are where you need to focus first.

Synthesis and Mobile Relevance

I've presented each of these use-cases in isolation, but that may not be the best way to think about them. You may want or need to address one of these use-cases specifically, which is fine, but you can also think about them as a matrix of attributes too. This approach may make more sense if you feel that you already have a foundation for your application, but you want to ensure that it is relevant for mobile space. Review your application in terms of the value that each of these cases represents. It's not necessary to address each one explicitly, you may find that there are aspects of one or more of these attributes that helps you focus your application in a way that improves it's relevance for mobile. You may find that in the process of doing this you may be able to create additional value and potentially carve out new, unidentified use-cases that will help increase the adoption of your application.

It's never a bad idea to be thinking through the general utility of your application by applying the concepts of Right Function and Task Efficiency. Depending on the nature of your app, these may not necessarily be the priority, but they are always applicable to one degree or another.

Location-based services should always be on the table too, whether this is the focus of your app or not. You need to ask yourself if there is a dimension of location functionality that can be applied to add value for the user while they are on the go.

Communication is another use-case that deserves consideration at a high level. This may be as simple as integrating "click to call" functionality in the appropriate place in your application, and communication complexity only goes up from there. Integration with social media is becoming increasingly important, both from a user's perspective and from a business perspective. This kind of one-to-many communication can be integrated in many different ways throughout an application. It's up to you to determine where and how to apply those types of functions, just know that your process for figuring that out should be driven by an explicit user need.

The degree to which you focus on various crossover use-cases is also somewhat dependent on device type. The bias of behavior types between the iPhone and iPad can help you understand how to best to support these use-cases in your application.

Translation into Mobile

I touched on the idea of translating existing applications, use-cases, and functionality a bit in the previous section, but it is a topic that's worth exploring a bit deeper because it is a common situation for many organizations.

If you are thinking about translating an application into the mobile space there are a few basic steps you should take to get started.

- **Identify your feature superset:** The application you may be translating may be functionally robust in its current state. Identify and list all the possible features.

- **Group and cluster:** Review your feature list and group or cluster like or related features together. You can also do this with a particular use-case or workflow in mind; just label and organize as needed.

- **Review and analyze:** Take a look at how your feature groupings are starting to resolve and look at if they are applicable to the mobile context at a high level, and if they may speak to specific use-case at a more detailed level.

- **Filter:** Remove or isolate features that are not relevant, based on the what you have identified as the primary use-cases from your user experience strategy and by what is appropriate or possible for the platform.

- **Identify areas of critical mass:** It may make sense to translate an application as a unified experience into a mobile app, but you should be looking at your grouped features to determine whether or not they can stand alone as applications unto themselves, and if it makes sense to fragment your application into multi-sub applications.

What I'm describing here is essentially a triage type effort that ultimately you would want to front load into your overall strategy. This won't give you all the answers, but it will help you ensure the relevance of your application for mobile users.

The last bullet really speaks to the optimization of user experience for more complex applications. High functional density is always a challenge for smaller-scale devices, not just in terms of UI mapping and layout, but because of the deeper hierarchical navigational structure that functional complexity implies. This may be less of an issue for a device like the iPad, but even there you may still have some significant challenges trying to replicate a desktop experience in a way that makes sense for the platform.

Summary

The notion of anytime, anywhere access to data and functionality is the core value of mobile computing. The fact that users are no longer limited to a fixed place and time to access a computing environment has radically changed how they think about what is possible. New use-cases and scenarios are emerging that are contributing to the accelerating adoption of devices like the iPhone.

There are nuances to mobile device behavior that will have an impact on design decisions for your application. Whereas the iPhone is a truly mobile platform, the iPad is not. We can differentiate between the two by stating that the iPad really represents more of a portable use-case because it is not universally present with the user, and it's use is often limited to situations where the user is stationary and prepared to be engaged for longer durations. iPhone usage is higher in frequency, but the engagement period is often very short. There are also differences in personal affinity between the two devices. Whereas the users have an extremely close affinity with their iPhones, the iPad has more opportunity to be a shared device.

I've identified five critical use-cases for mobile:

- Communication
- Entertainment
- Location-Based Services
- Commerce
- Utility

These use-cases cover a wide array of applications and functions. They should be used to either identify areas of opportunity, or they can be used to help increase the relevance and add value to an existing application as it is transitioned into the mobile space.

Translating existing applications into mobile can be challenging, but there five simple tasks you can perform to help make this transition seamless and drive relevance for mobile uses.

Addressing mobile use-cases from this perspective will have a significant impact on improving your user experience and will help ensure that your application is useful, relevant, and engaging.

Leveraging iOS Capabilities for Optimal User Experience

Apple's iOS is a fantastic platform to design for. Out of all the mobile platforms on the market today, it provides the best support for the rendering of user experience and all the highly nuanced visual interaction that often entails. Apple has done an excellent job of providing a variety of specialized technologies to enable a development team to overcome even the most complex challenges that a designer can bring to the table.

There's been much discussion in the interaction design community around the notion of "designer-developer workflow." Many of the new technologies driving contemporary web user experience provide a seamless transition for design material moving between the design and development domains. This has had the effect of making the creation of sophisticated user experiences a much more streamlined affair, with less communication overhead for teams and greater design fidelity for the experiences being created. Additionally, there has been a revolutionary shift in traditional project roles as more designers move beyond just the specification of user experience, and begin to directly implement front-end code.

There's been a recognition within project teams that it's extremely valuable to have design staff that possess a working knowledge of the technologies being used to implement their work. In reality this needs to be more than just a basic familiarity with ideas and terminology. In an ideal situation, a designer would be intimately familiar with the strengths and weaknesses of a particular technology and be able to design a solution that takes those capabilities into account. This implies that it may be necessary for a designer to have firsthand knowledge of a specific technology. It's not reasonable to expect that a designer, or design team, has robust development skills and extensive experience coding for a particular platform. However, if a designer has either experimented with a technology on their own, or as a part of an internal training initiative, they can be much more efficient when designing a viable solution. Even just taking a day to review any supporting documentation applicable to the execution of front-end experience can help ensure a more streamlined development effort. If that documentation is not immediately understood, designers should work with their development team to help identify all the key software issues that may influence design execution. This all speaks to the need for designers to start thinking about themselves as technologists, wherein they establish themselves as experts on the primary technologies used to manifest the experiences that they are working hard to define.

With all of that said, I'm going to walk through the core technologies responsible for delivering visual interaction within iOS. Each one of these has specific capabilities and design benefits that I will review. As you start to think about your user experience, keep these technologies in the back of your mind and consider how each may help you accomplish your design goals.

Beyond that I'm going to review a few other iOS platform-related topics important for every designer to know. Most of these are recurring topics that seem to pop up during any initial discussion about the creation of an iPhone or iPad application. These topics will revolve around custom skinning, iPhone and iPad development support, and understanding the user experience implications of native app capabilities versus mobile web capabilities.

Key Technologies

I've identified four key technologies that you need to be aware of as a designer. These can be broken down and grouped into two basic categories, the first being Apple technologies which support native rendering within iOS, and the second being OpenGL, a third-party technology that supports low-level GPU usage. The best way to think about this from a design standpoint is to associate native rending with the presentation of classic user interface widgets as they are commonly understood. Associate OpenGL with high-performance graphics rendering for the kinds of animation and interaction that you might see in a gaming context.

The important thing to note is that these technologies do not have to be exclusively applied to the original contexts for which they were intended. By understanding the nature of each of these technologies you can understand how the experience you are designing can be best brought to life. This will become increasingly important as you begin to think through the details of unique interaction mechanics as they may be applied to your application. When you know what each of these technologies enables, you will see just how powerful iOS is and the unlimited possibilities iOS gives you as a designer.

UIKit

UIKit is the meat and potatoes framework used to flesh out the application experience for any iOS device. It essentially provides all the tools and resources to assemble a user interface for a touch screen device and as such, accounts for all the critical points of user interaction that your application might need.

In all likelihood UIKit will deliver 95% of the user experience that you are trying to create. The framework encompasses all the UI widgets that you typically encounter while using an iOS device. This includes basic button controls, sliders, text fields, toggle controls, and the like. Along with the standard control appearances that we are all familiar with, UIKit provides plenty of opportunities to customize objects as needed, so never feel constrained by what is provided by default. Customized UI solutions that use the other graphics technologies I'll be reviewing will all ultimately be managed by UIKit, so it is an extremely flexible framework and worth getting to know.

Besides being able to consume any production graphics (i.e., raster objects like PNG files) that you specify in your designs, UIkit has the ability to render objects procedurally. In other words it can draw objects as needed and as specified. These techniques are more akin to many of the vector graphics methods that you might already be familiar with. In most cases this will involve the definition of some basic geometry or path, and the application of visual attributes to those paths to achieve the appearance you desire. Just a word of warning for those of you considering this option: Although the use of procedural graphics will streamline your production effort for application assets, you will need to spend a considerable amount of time with the development team defining attributes and making sure objects are rendering as you need them to. Depending on the nature of the experience you would like to create, it may be more effective to render certain UI elements in this way. You'll need to work with your development partners to decide where and when procedural techniques make the most sense.

Core Graphics

Core Graphics is another really interesting technology that may be used to add value to your user experience. At the heart of Core Graphics is the two-dimensional rendering engine called Quartz 2D which can be used to drive many different kinds of graphics capabilities within an application. Not only can it be used to draw certain kinds of graphics dynamically, but it can be used as a fully featured imaging engine to add graphic creation and editing capabilities to an app.

Think of Core Graphics fundamentally as a technology that lets you expand the functionality of an application. However, because it provides more complex graphics support than what is available in UIKit, it can be used to create user interface elements if needed. Considering that UIKit enables a high degree of flexibility for the support of custom graphics, Core Graphics may only be useful if the experience that you are designing demands some kind of complex graphic transform, processing, or realtime compositing.

Core Animation

Core Animation is a technology dedicated to giving developers a simple and easy solution for the creation and rendering of dynamic visual interaction attributes. In other words, it's all about bringing your user experience to life.

Because it is focused on integration of animation into existing user interface objects, Core Animation works in close conjunction with UIKit, so the integration of reactive controls and transitions is relatively seamless.

Core Animation is actually quite a powerful tool in terms of the range of capabilities that it gives to developers. We've all experienced the beautiful state transitions common to many applications, but don't think that you are limited to what you can do based on what you've seen in other applications so far. This technology gives developers the ability to create and control animatable attributes at many different levels, so you, as the designer should consider that the possibilities for unique and highly customized animation are virtually unlimited.

OpenGL ES

OpenGL ES stands out from the other technologies that I've reviewed here in that it is the only non-Apple technology in use. OpenGL ES is essentially the API that let's you tap into the hardware acceleration embedded in iOS devices for the rendering of graphics. It cannot stand alone to deliver a user experience per se, but must be used in conjunction with Core Animation to deliver content to the screen.

Again, this is another powerful technology that is used to render graphics that might otherwise be extremely taxing for the device to manage. For the most part, OpenGL ES is used in the gaming context when 3D objects need to be rendered on the fly. However, because of it's integration with the other technologies above, do not consider it limited to the rendering of game graphics. It is entirely possible to render UI objects, or even an entire application within a three-dimensional (3D) environment if desired.

The need to integrate this technology with your application will be entirely dependent on the types of visuals you are trying to produce. There are many ways to create the appearance of 3D graphics without needing to render objects on the fly. Unless you have designed an experience that requires real-time reactivity with 3D objects in an unconstrained 3D space, you may want to consider some other options. On the other hand, you may want to experiment with this technology just to understand new types of visual interaction that may not be fully explored or developed yet. In which case, this technology will give you some very interesting capabilities to experiment with.

Custom Skinning

Maybe the section title should read, "To Custom Skin or Not To Custom Skin" because that seems to be a perennial question when considering the creation of an iPhone or iPad app. I think that this question may have been more common when the App Store originally launched. In a rush to get something into the App Store, product managers seemed to be willing to forego any significant design activities in an effort to compress development schedules. This is not so much the case now, but this still seems to be an issue for many organizations dipping their toes into the App Store for the first time.

Understanding the value of a customized visual appearance can be a hurdle for some teams to get over. However, the rationale for making the decision to create and use customized assets is fairly simple. Building an application using the default objects provided by the SDK means that you will be using Apple's visual identity to create your app. Your users will essentially have an Apple experience when all is said and done. This isn't a bad thing, but if you want your experience to be recognizably representative of your own brand then this is probably not the right path to take.

Apart from any philosophical or strategic reason to avoid a custom design solution, from what I've described so far, there really is no technical reason to avoid the integration of custom graphics throughout your app. Apple gives developers a number of different methods by which to do so and custom graphics are natural part of the overall development workflow.

To be clear, this really isn't a black and white discussion. You can integrate custom graphics in every area of your application, but that doesn't mean that you have to customize everything. There will be situations where it may make more sense to leverage what the SDK provides by default. However, the design system as a whole will need to account for how you manage the integration of default controls with controls that have a custom appearance. This is not a technical issue, but rather one of user perception. You just need to make sure that the user does not see customized controls as being something apart from controls with a standard appearance, unless that is the effect you are trying to achieve.

Beyond the simple re-skinning of common controls with new graphics, you also have the ability to design and create entirely new UI objects that support unique input and interaction. This isn't so much about re-skinning as it is about wholesale reinvention. The HIG discourages this to a degree, not because it is difficult and time consuming to do, but because it introduces a barrier to understanding if the user has never encountered the control before. Generally speaking, that is good guidance, but the success or failure of a reinvented control is really only dependent on the design solution itself. Cryptic design solutions are obviously going to frustrate users no matter how cool they look, but an elegant solution that is easily identifiable in it's operation will not be a problem.

Universal Considerations

The evolution and expansion of iOS devices over the past few years has created a shifting landscape that has presented a number of challengers for app designers and developers to contend with. Early on life was simple; we only had to design a solution for one device. With the introduction of the iPad things got a bit more complicated and we had to figure out how to put all that extra screen real estate to use. Design challenges notwithstanding, this presented a difficult situation for development teams because their efforts were essentially doubled when the need arose to deploy two apps simultaneously.

Recently we've seen the introduction of Universal Apps within the app store. These are applications that can be run on any iOS device because they contain the necessary code to render the UI for both contexts. Universal Apps automatically know what device they are being run on and can reflect changes in the user experience accordingly. This is not only true for how the UI is rendered, but also by what functionality is available on the device.

From a development perspective this is great news because this introduces significant efficiencies into the development process. From a design perspective you will still have to define precisely what those two different experiences are and make sure that your design solutions are appropriate for their respective platforms. However, knowing that you may be designing for two platforms simultaneously does provide some distinct advantages. Instead of trying to retrofit a design into a new platform (going either way) and thinking through how various design elements and interactions will be mapped in, you can account for appropriate consistency and appropriate variation up front. This approach can be important if you are targeting users who may experience your application on both devices.

App versus Mobile Web Considerations

There can be a lot of debate within organizations about the actual need for a native iOS application. With the current fragmentation of the mobile market it can be very challenging to dedicate resources to the creation of native applications for every relevant platform. For many, a mobile web experience is a viable solution to this problem. However, there are many significant issues associated with a mobile web solution that must be considered before moving forward.

The first issue that must be recognized is the fact that there is a lack of parity between experiences delivered by the web and those rendered natively on the device. Although there are many technologies capable of rendering fairly compelling user experiences within the browser environment, none of them compare to what can be done in the native context. As I've reviewed before, Apple gives you access to some very powerful technologies that not only allow you to deliver highly customized and unique interactions, but it delivers those interactions at an unparalleled level of performance. A mobile web solution can only provide support for a limited subset of visual interactions that a native experience can deliver, and it does so at a fraction of the performance that a native app can provide. This isn't necessarily a negative point, you'll just have to make sure that your design solution is accounting for these limitations.

I should also point out that the native versus mobile web argument is really not an either/or situation. The nature of iOS is such that these experiences can be hybridized. A user experience for a native application may span both native elements and web-based elements as a single cohesive experience. This allows you, when needed, to access to best of both worlds: the power and dynamism of native UI rendering and the flexibility and ease of maintenance of web-based experiences.

Your solution will ultimately depend on the functional requirements of your application and the desired user experience needed to manifest those functions. Any discussion about the implementation of your application experience should be done from that perspective first, and not because of any arbitrary bias toward one technology or another.

Summary

Apple provides four key technologies for delivering the interactions that drive the user experience of applications:

- **UIKit:** This is the framework that will be responsible for delivering the vast majority of your user experience.

- **Core Graphics:** A two-dimensional rendering engine that can add graphic creation and editing functionality to an app. It may also be used to support the rendering of user interface elements when appropriate.

- **Core Animation:** Core Animation works closely with UIKit to add dynamic visual interaction to user interface elements.

- **OpenGL ES:** A third-party technology that taps into the integrated hardware acceleration embedded in iOS devices. OpenGL ES provides high-performance graphics capabilities for 2D and 3D object rendering.

With all of the graphics capabilities inherent to iOS, do not be afraid to customize graphics, design unique interactions, or experiment with object behaviors.

Apple now gives you the ability to combine iPhone and iPad user experiences into a single application to simplify deployment and maintenance. However, you will still need to undertake design efforts to define the two different user experiences. The main design advantage being the ability to define greater UX continuity for both devices up front, as opposed to retrofitting one design solution to another device.

Interaction Modeling and the Creation of Novel Concepts

This chapter really gets to the heart of what this book is about. Up to this point I have provided the background information necessary for understanding the design decisions that will determine the user experience of your application. The questions now are, how do you go about making the design decisions that will differentiate your application from those of your competitors, and how do you arrive at the breakthrough ideas that will set you apart? This chapter will walk you through the basic process, the key points of consideration, and the critical techniques that will ultimately get you the Wow factor that you seek.

This is not a simple formula, and you will not automatically arrive at a magical and amazing application when you are done. The process requires hard work, analytical thinking, and a touch of creativity. If you are willing to provide all of that, you have a great shot a creating a breakthrough application.

What Is Wow?

We need to start by trying to define what "Wow factor" actually is. The term is not really a working concept in the design lexicon; rather, it's an expression of users' favorable reaction to a unique or especially engaging application. While the use of this term may be problematic from a design perspective, it does a decent job of reflecting the gut response that users experience, and it is generally a reaction that we can all relate to at one level or another. But that still doesn't answer the question.

In relation to the interaction of an iOS app, Wow factor can be defined as being an expression of the engagement layer of your application when that engagement exceeds a critical emotional threshold for the user. That threshold is ultimately dependent on the user, and as such is difficult to predict or determine without clearly understanding the personas to be targeted. However, we can discuss the nature of that emotional threshold and the key factors needed for that threshold to be crossed. These factors are as follows:

- **Immediacy of impact:** A design must be able to elicit an immediate response from the user.

- **Recognition of novelty or identifiable difference:** A user must be able to recognize the novelty of a given design, or at least identify it as being different from a more conventional experience.

- **Positive response:** There must be an inherent appeal to the solution that mitigates the shock of a potentially strange or foreign experience.

When these three factors are in place the user will easily cross the emotional threshold required to achieve the affective quality of Wow.

It's important to recognize that the idea of Wow and the contributing factors that determine it can be influenced by the attributes exhibited by a particular design solution. These attributes often work in concert toward a greater effect and often are not solely responsible for creating the response that you want.

However, we can isolate these attributes in order to identify their unique contributions to user experience:

- **Appearance:** This describes the cosmetic attributes of a given design solution as expressed through the screen structure, layout, rendering, and other elements comprising the static-state visuals of an app.

- **Interaction mechanics and behavior:** This refers to the physical interaction, unique gestures, and general input required to engage with the user interface elements of an application.

- **Visual interaction, motion, and animation:** These refer to the reactive or dynamic elements of a design solution that bring it to life. These may be closely associated with a particular interaction through feedback or reactivity to user input, but this also accounts for ambient qualities within a design, or even transitory states not directly related to an interaction.

It is possible to achieve a Wow reaction by focusing on only one of these dimensions and executing it very well. There are certainly examples out there where this is the case. An application may lack any kind of compelling interactivity, but may be so beautiful in its appearance that the other attributes don't factor into a user's perception in any appreciable way. On the other hand, an application may have a minimal appearance that on its own has no overt visual appeal, yet it may also offer such compelling interaction mechanics or visual interaction characteristics that it achieves the desired response from the user on those attributes alone.

It is a high-risk proposition to depend on a single attribute to get you across that emotional threshold with users. It's important to note that the three attributes just described are not necessarily equally weighted when it comes to iOS devices. An attractive-looking application is a table stakes proposition for the user, so it will be difficult to exceed their expectations on this front. Additionally, there is nothing inherent to the iOS platform that presents a differentiated means of experiencing the visual nature of your app. While their displays are fantastic compared with other smart phones, they are not significantly different from a decent-quality desktop display.

The attributes that provide the most opportunity for Wow are the interaction mechanics and behavior inherent to your application experience. This is based on the fact that iOS devices provide methods of control and interaction that are fundamentally different from other types of digital experiences that the user might be familiar with. As I discussed in Chapter 3, users have a desire to experience something new and different with these devices, and by paying close attention to interaction mechanics, you can give them the experience they want.

However, bearing in mind that the interaction mechanics of an app is the attribute to focus on, you still can't ignore appearance and visual interaction since they are all part of the same experiential continuum. The main point is that you should focus on mechanics or behavior first, and that will help inform how you solve for the other two remaining attributes.

Interaction Modeling: Process Overview

Interaction modeling is a method by which you can formulate fundamental interaction mechanics and key visual interactions that will serve as the basis for your application experience. The interaction modeling process is composed of four key tasks, three of which are necessary precursor activities and the fourth is the interaction modeling itself. I walk through each of these at a high level first before diving into the details of the modeling considerations, tasks, and examples.

Requirements Definition

To start with, there must be at least some rudimentary understanding of the functional requirements of your application. These may be expressed as part of your user experience strategy or captured in detail as a part of a formalized requirements specification. This information forms the basis for all of your design activities moving forward, so you need to make sure that it is in a stable state and firmly agreed upon by the team. If you work within a more Agile environment there is an assumption that this information may be a bit less fixed, but you should still have a critical mass of requirements defining the functionality before you begin your work. With requirements in hand, you can begin to craft the appropriate use-cases.

Use-Case and Scenario Development

Use-cases, especially those that are more scenario-driven, are an important part of the process. A good use-case should provide the team with a sense of the general workflow that a user will experience as well as an understanding of how various requirements are intended to be addressed within a context of use. Some use-cases may provide explicit guidance through the narrative of a scenario that describes key interactions at various points in the application experience. Keep in mind that a use-case, expressed as a scenario or not, is intended to be just a starting point. If you have a vision for your application and how it may express behavior to the user, then you can describe it to the level of detail you think will be helpful for informing the later stages of the process. If you don't have those details at this point that's not really an issue, provided you can describe the general activities undertaken by the user. With this in place you can move on to the next step.

Application Workflow

There are many different ways to address the workflow of an application and each has its own unique purpose and value. From a design standpoint we are more concerned with workflow that identifies the decision logic, key interaction points, and navigational constructs required to move the user from point A to B. This is a user-centric view that defines the structure of an application by establishing the relationships of features and functionality as they are presented to the user. A well-defined workflow gives you an accurate map of your application, but it does not make any assumptions about the mechanics of the interactions that may drive it, or how functionality will be presented.

Interaction Modeling

This is where the rubber meets the road. Once you understand the basic workflow of your application and how those functional relationships are conceptually organized you can begin thinking through how these points of interaction are presented to the user.

Interaction modeling defines the gross behavior of the application with the core interactions required of the user to accomplish the key tasks identified in your workflow. This may include management of screen real estate through visual user interface modalities (such as functional shifts driven by device orientation), the presentation of navigation, fundamental gestures, and any other information pertaining to the general operation of the user interface. To put it another way, interaction modeling defines how your application will operate, without determining specifically what the application will do.

It's through this activity that you can begin to craft the experience of your application. One workflow could spawn an infinite number of different interaction models, each functionally similar but with radically different experience layered into the application. You'll see examples of this later in this chapter.

Process Details

Now I'll take you through the details of process, from thinking through your workflow, working out an interaction model, problem solving techniques, and more details on how to set the user experience you create apart from the crowd through the crafting of signature interaction.

Thinking Through Workflow

The definition of workflow is the essence of all interaction design activities. It is where you specify how the user will interact with your application. The problem is, workflow definition can be done at many different levels depending on what you are trying to achieve. There are circumstances where you may only need to define workflow in the most abstract sense, ignoring functional details and the specific interactions that may drive them. This may be valuable for mapping out the relationships of feature clusters and the general flow between them. On the opposite end of the spectrum are situations where you may need to define the logic of all interactions, events, and state changes the user may experience in an effort to provide a very clear picture of the operation of your application.

For the purpose of the interaction modeling activities you want to have more detail than an abstract, high-level workflow, though you may not need to get too highly detailed either. The level of detail required for fleshing out your interaction model varies according to the nature of your application.

Working Out an Interaction Model

As I stated previously, interaction modeling is about working through concepts that define the gross behavior of the application and understanding how those gross behaviors may be applied or formulated to create a consistent and understandable model for the user. In Chapter 2 I reviewed "The Strange Topology of iOS," which broke down the conceptual model and spatial model that are fundamental to the iOS user experience. The idea of the layered planes and the spatial model that the user moves through are what constitute the basic interaction model for iOS as a whole, and you can see from that example how powerful that thinking can be when approached in the right way (see Figure 6-1).

Figure 6-1. The iOS spatial model as experienced on an iPhone

Getting started with interaction modeling requires you to start thinking in a deliberately abstract way. Without getting into the specifics of functionality or content, you need to think through the different behaviors that might be employed by your app to get an idea about how they may be used to control elements on the screen. iOS gives you an incredible palette of options to begin working with. Ideas like zoom, pan, flicking, sliding, and scrolling can all be applied to interesting effect, either by themselves or as compound effects to create some very different interactions.

I've talked a lot about differentiation up to this point, and one of the biggest challenges that you will face is figuring out where and how to best differentiate the interactions contained within your app. Understanding how these types of ideas can be used is the essential benefit of interaction modeling; it's the point where you are free to experiment and think through how those ideas can be applied to your design problem. Arriving at a differentiated solution is not all that difficult, but creating a solution that is scalable, extensible, and most importantly, understood by the user, takes a bit more effort.

Let's do a quick little exercise to understand how to break out of the box and think through some differentiated interactions. Start by thinking about a simple user interface widget; say, a list of items. List objects are fairly common to any user experience or user interface design effort and can be used for a number of purposes. Traditionally, a list is a vertical arrangement of text objects, where each text object is clearly delineated from the objects above and below it within a single column (see Figure 6-2).

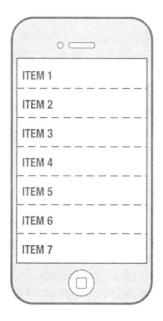

Figure 6-2. A typical list

Take a step back now and think about what a list is in the most abstract sense. It's basically just an array of objects from which you can make a selection. It's a pretty basic idea if you think about it. However, if you think about it some more, you'll see that there's nothing inherently critical to it being vertically arranged, nor is there any inherent value to it being organized in a single column. So you have to ask yourself, is there is an alternative format that can add value to the problem you are trying to solve? This may not be readily apparent, so it's worth thinking through the options to see if anything interesting arises. For the purposes of this exercise let's take a look at how this might play out.

If we know or even just believe there's no inherent value in the vertical aspect of a list, what would a horizontal solution look like (see Figure 6-3)?

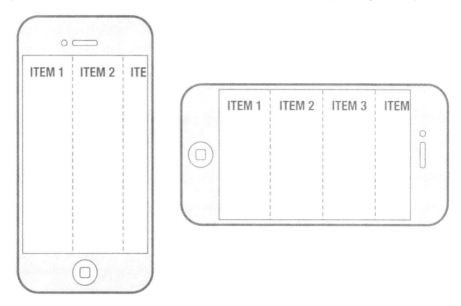

Figure 6-3. Experimental horizontal list options

OK, this is interesting, but we can begin to see that there may be some issues with the amount of horizontal real estate available to us when the device is being held vertically. Is this a huge problem? Outside of any specific context, no, but it may not be very efficient for quick browsing given that you can't see as many list items at once. It works a little better when the device is oriented horizontally, but it's still not ideal.

Let's expand our thinking a bit and see where that takes us. The notion of a single column of list objects could be questioned too. If we expanded a list to be an array of objects or some kind of grid configuration, what advantages does that give us (see Figure 6-4)?

Figure 6-4. Rethinking a list as a grid or array of objects

This is now starting to get a bit more interesting. This configuration provides the advantage of being able to view many things simultaneously, which seems to be an improvement over a more conventional list. There are some drawbacks that we have to contend with here too. The amount of available area for the text objects is diminished, but that appears to manageable if we are willing to change the size of the text objects.

Wow! We started with just the basic idea of the list and look where we ended up. With just some simple experimentation we were able to radically transform the basic idea of the widget. The development of this idea doesn't need to end here, either; there are other dimensions we can begin to explore as well. Let's think about the interaction behaviors associated with lists and list-type objects. In iOS a classic list object can be navigated with a quick flick up or down, or a slow drag to scroll to items beyond the boundaries of the screen. Is this behavior still relevant, and can it be applied to our grid experiment (see Figure 6-5)?

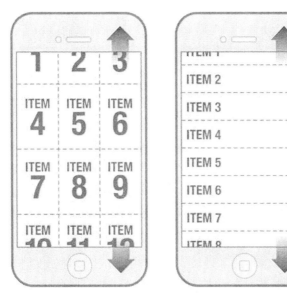

Figure 6-5. Vertical scrolling applies to both solutions

Sure it can! In this particular case the applicability of scrolling behavior is common sense, but that won't always be the case. You will always need to evaluate the extant behavior of the interaction you are building upon to make sure that it is still valid within the new model.

We're still not done with this example. Now let's apply the abstraction method to the behavior of the list. A standard iOS list object supports scrolling when needed, and that scrolling is limited to a single axis because of the orientation of the text objects in a vertical column. Given that we are no longer limiting ourselves to single vertical column of items, how can we apply scrolling behavior to this basic concept?

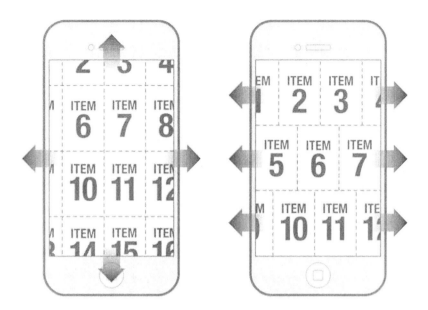

Figure 6-6. Multi-axis scrolling & row scrolling on a grid

There are many ways scrolling behavior can be applied to this concept, all of which may be equally valid (see Figure 6-6). You can see from this series of examples how easy it is to formulate new ideas based on existing widgets and interactions. Using a list as your inspiration is just a start; there are many other ideas, widgets, and other elements that can be used in the same way. Deconstructing these can be a powerful way to design and flesh out some very compelling interactions for your application.

Additional Problem-Solving Techniques

We've just walked through the process of deriving a new concept from a fairly basic control. This is a great technique to get started on defining a new interaction model for your application, but it may not get you to the end point that you need. At some point in the process you will encounter potential dead-ends. A particular technique or format may not scale to the degree that you expected it to, or you might find that one of the positive aspects of your solution winds up boxing you in when applied to other areas of an application. In those situations you need some basic problem-solving techniques to help you think yourself back out of the corner.

We've talked about the amazing capabilities that iOS provides to help designers create amazing user experiences. One of the most powerful technologies is Core Animation, which gives developers the tools to integrate highly customized animations throughout an application. Animation is not just about applying whiz-bang motion to random elements for a specific visual effect; it is also an incredibly powerful tool for communication.

To understand how animation can be of value to us, let's breakdown what animation is. At the most basic level, animation is the ability to change or alter the attributes or characteristics of an object over time. The key idea here is time. Time is one of the most powerful tools you can bring to bear to resolve key interaction design problems.

Time becomes extremely useful in situations when you have a limited amount of space. When space is constrained, it can be very difficult to communicate complex ideas or display complex information. Two situations arise when working within constrained space. You end up with either an extremely high level of information density, or you end up truncating or reducing the amount of information to fit within the available space. Both scenarios are problematic. Extremely dense information can be difficult for a user to consume and comprehend. Truncated information is incomplete, and will not satisfactorily resolve the design need or requirement.

Our list experiment does a great job of demonstrating this. In order to make the text work within a grid unit we just scaled it down to the point where it would fit and still be legible. But obviously, if we didn't scale it, we'd have the situation illustrated next (see Figure 6-7).

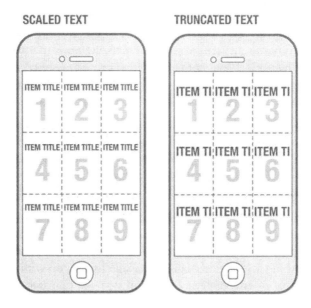

Figure 6-7. Scaled text compared to truncated text within a grid of selectable objects

The example with the scaled text is somewhat successful, but clearly the example with the truncated text is not a desirable solution. Let's assume for the sake of this example that scaling the text to fit within the grid element is not something that we want to pursue. How can time be applied to help resolve the issue of text string length? We can look back to the day of small-screen smartphones and feature phones for the answer.

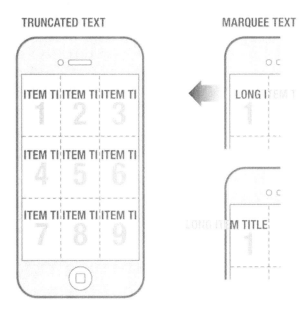

Figure 6-8. Truncated text compared to marquee text moving through the viewable region of grid element

Marquee text used to be quite a popular solution a few years back. Time comes into play here because the solution animates the text through the viewable area over time. As the text marches from right to left the user can read the entire string (see Figure 6-8). This resolves the issue of truncation. The introduction of time, as an additional dimension to work with, provides one way to resolve the issue of constrained space.

This is an interesting solution that might be applicable in certain situations, but for a couple of reasons it's not an ideal solution for this grid layout. Imagine this screen loading for the first time, with text panning and within every grid unit. It's safe to say that you would be overwhelmed with the on-slaught of animated text. It would be a challenge to focus on an individual grid element, and you would have to deliberately time the viewing of a grid element to watch a single text string cycle from beginning to end. Otherwise, you end up with the same problem seen with the truncated text, where only a snippet of each string is visible. What is the missing element here? The missing element is user control, which can come into a play in a number of different ways.

The idea of user control is obvious given that the thrust of this discussion is how to create an interaction design solution, and you certainly cannot have interaction without some form of user control (not for the purposes of this experiment, at any rate; in Chapter 8 I'll address how this might not necessarily be the case). But here I want you to think about user control in a slightly different way, through the idea of "state."

State is a very important idea when it comes to thinking through a potential interaction model. It is another problem-solving technique that can be applied to problematic areas of a design solution. Much like time, state opens up possibilities that would otherwise be impossible in a static solution. In a sense, state—like time—can be thought of as another dimension that allows you to modify elements and information being managed on screen.

What exactly is state? State refers to all the extant properties, characteristics, and attributes of an object as they are observed by a user and/or managed by the controlling system.

Up to this point we have been thinking about our emerging interaction model for our evolved list solution with only a single state defined. That is, it only has one form, and that form does not change. But this doesn't have to be the case. If we can manipulate state and change the construct of our model, then we should be able to resolve any of the problematic areas that we observe in our interaction model.

To link this back to the idea of user control, we can say that we have the ability to instance different states of a user interface through the mechanism of user input.

So, how can we apply the ideas of user control and state to resolve the issues inherent to our experiment in interaction modeling? We left off with a solution that had a few different issues. We liked the efficiency that the grid provided for displaying a greater quantity of text items, but by increasing the number of items in the list we started to compromise the amount of real estate available for the display of text. We experimented with a time-based solution, but there were some idiosyncrasies associated with applying animation universally to the grid. With this in mind, let's look at a similar solution that integrates user control.

SWIPE TO REVEAL

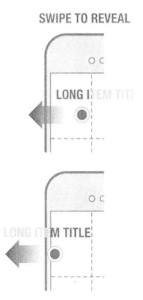

Figure 6-9. Swiping to reveal hidden text

This technique leverages the concept of direct manipulation to allow the user to expose more text when and where they choose. Instead of being confronted with a screen full of animated text strings, the user can now take action and read whichever portions of text are desired (see Figure 6-9).

Applying some interactivity to a text object is a solution that works, but it's a relatively simple one. What if we expand that thinking to arrive at something a bit more revolutionary? Instead of concerning ourselves with the text object by itself, let's think about the entire grid unit and how that might change state with a user's input.

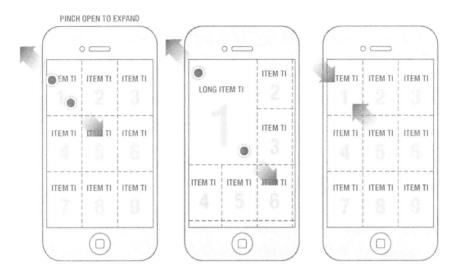

Figure 6-10. Pinching open a grid element to reveal more information, then snapping back to size

Now we have an interaction that demonstrates a higher degree of dynamism in the model. With a simple gesture, the user can expand a grid element to create a larger area in which to view information (see Figure 6-10). Not only is the text object readable in its entirety, but there's now more area that we can populate with additional value-added information.

What was once just an idea around a basic list, is now a potentially very compelling user experience. From my perspective this aspect of the model appears to add some practical utility—probably more than just the ability to expose a text string. But why and how can we take advantage of this?

One of the main things to be aware of when undertaking a process like this is that you need to avoid thinking about these ideas in a vacuum. An interaction model is a model of a complete system, a system that defines the operation of your application. If you believe that you have an interaction concept that is robust enough to drive your application, then you need to think about how that concept can be mapped into the other aspects of the user experience. This is what I referred to earlier in this chapter when I addressed issue of scalability and extensibility. If you have a compelling interaction that is not applicable to other aspects of your application, that's OK. You may have a larger interaction model in mind that can encapsulate that concept and provide a clear and coherent model for the user. However, an application with many unique interactions—each specialized and different from the next—does nothing but confuse and frustrate the user. In effect, that approach accomplishes precisely the opposite of what you set out to do. You won't have an interaction model at that point, just an agglomeration of odd interactions.

Avoiding that situation requires you to continually think through the applicability of your interaction across a large swath of your app. This is a form of systems-level thinking that will serve your application extremely well. The key to understanding the applicability of a given interaction across multiple contexts requires you to elevate your thinking to an abstract level. You need to view your interaction not for the immediate solution that it provides, but rather for the basic behavior that the interaction illustrates and the possibilities of what that may enable. Think of your interaction as a basic behavioral template or pattern that can be used in multiple places and in multiple ways.

The fewer the unique behavioral instances and interactions you use to formulate your application, the more robust your interaction model will be. Less is definitely more when it comes to designing your application. Your goal should always be to reduce the overall cognitive load for the user by leveraging their knowledge and experience with the interaction patterns they have already encountered in the application.

However, you don't want to force yourself to use a behavior or pattern where it doesn't make sense. It can be very tempting to map your established interactions across all aspects of your user experience, but you'll know when this isn't working when you find yourself spending an inordinate amount of time trying to resolve a design solution for a particular problem. If the solution isn't patently obvious to you, then it likely will not be obvious to the user, either.

As you may have noticed, I've use the concepts of interaction, behavior, and pattern interchangeably. I think of these terms as having a distinct relationship to one another that should probably be clarified.

■ **Interaction:** I view this as the unit level of interactivity, such as the click of a button or a swipe across the screen. It's essentially the action taken for input by the user as prompted by the system.

■ **Behavior:** This is second order of complexity arising from the input of the user and the resulting feedback of the system. It is the perceived gestalt effect of interaction as demonstrated by the system.

■ **Pattern:** I defined this as the cumulative effect of compound behaviors working in a predicable and well-organized manner.

Your interaction model may seek to develop consistency at any one of these levels. This can be accomplished by leveraging large-scale patterns across the board, or by taking a more granular approach and ensuring interaction-level consistency with the objects that populate your application. Your effort in interaction modeling will determine the right approach for your particular situation.

Crafting Signature Interaction

The idea of actively seeking to differentiate from potential competitors leads naturally to the discussion of "signature interaction." A signature interaction is an interaction that is uniquely and deliberately identifiable with your application, your brand, or your organization. Moving to create a signature interaction is a strategic decision that needs to be determined as a part of your overall user experience strategy. Essentially, everything covered thus far regarding the methods applied to interaction modeling can also be used to define a signature interaction.

Getting to a signature interaction isn't about applying additional techniques to the overall process, it's more of a mindset and design goal for the resulting solution. By seeking to differentiate you are already looking to define a signature interaction, but up to this point all of this has been thought through only for a single application. If your organization is small and your product portfolio is limited to one app, then you are on the right track. If you are part of an organization with more than one product in its portfolio, then you need to expand your system-level thinking to encompass other applications and their functionality. What this means is that you need to increase the scope of your problem solving during the interaction modeling activities such that you understand the impact of your decision across a family of applications.

If we take a look at the interaction modeling example we have worked out so far, we could say that the grid unit expansion and the correlated gesture driving it might be suitable as a signature interaction. So far we've only thought in terms of resolving the text object truncation problem, but let's think through some options as they may be applied to a more generalized concept. Assuming that we are now thinking through an app, how and where else could this interaction be put to work? One option would be to consider it for navigation. Let's say that the grid array of items represents major functional nodes in the application. Could we use the idea of expansion and exposition of the grid unit as mechanism for navigation? Of course.

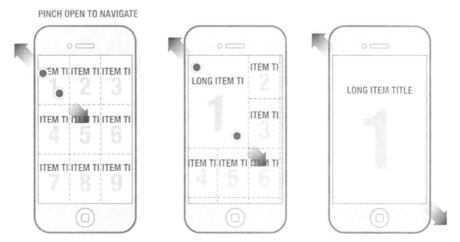

Figure 6-11. Using a pinch open to select and navigate. Past a certain threshold, the grid element continues to open up unaided by the user.

The basic idea here is the notion of expansion. A user can expand a grid unit with the spread of the fingers to reveal more information concealed within the unit (see Figure 6-11). If the user does not exceed a predetermined threshold of expansion, the grid unit would snap back to its original size when the user's fingers are removed from the screen. If the user expands the grid element past the predetermined threshold the grid unit then automatically expands to the full size of the screen and displays the functionality of that node (or becomes a gateway to sub-nodes, for that matter). A conventional approach to navigation would likely just require the user to touch one of the grid units to navigate to its corresponding node in the app. I think we can assume that we'd support that as well and assume that a quick tap has the same effect of expanding a grid unit past the threshold.

We're now starting to establish a distinct interaction model for the application. Instead of presenting a linear spatial model with both discrete and contiguous node-like experiences like that of the OS layer of the iPhone, we now have a spatial model defined by the elasticity of certain key regions. The user doesn't navigate by moving from point A to point B within the app, but instead exposes functionality where and when it's needed. From a workflow perspective there's no difference between the two, but from an experiential perspective the difference is radical.

Documentation

Documenting an interaction model is an important part of the process. You will want to capture your ideas so that they can be shared and communicated to other members of your design and development team. This will help ensure that your vision is well-understood when it comes time to execute the concepts as more detailed user interface deliverables.

Your documentation can take any form that you like. You just need to make sure that you account for two basic things:

- Demonstrate the nature of your interaction model visually, in a clear and concise manner.

- Provide extensive notation for the details of your interaction model that cannot be easily communicated visually.

Remember, what you are showing is not an explicit user interface treatment or the mapping of controls like you might see in a wireframe. This kind of deliverable intentionally lacks the level of detail that you would explore in your wireframe documentation. The focus of the interaction model is only to describe the gross behavior of the application such that you can move into more detailed interaction design activities with a clear vision.

Here's an example of how this documentation might look for the example that we worked through (see Figure 6-12).

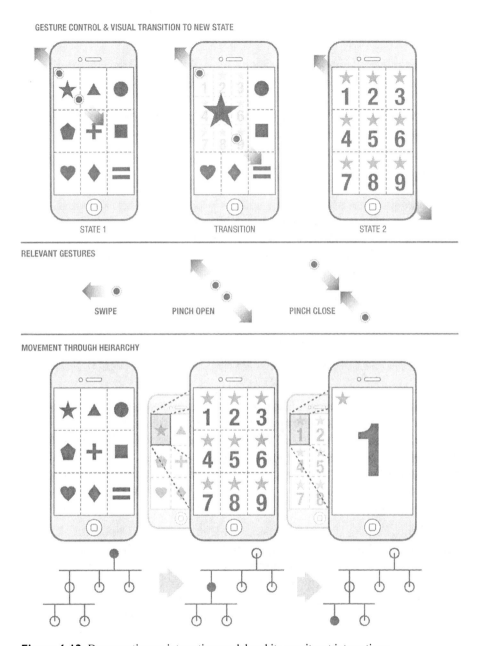

Figure 6-12. Documenting an interaction model and its consituent interactions

Case Study and Example

In order to understand how these ideas can be applied to a design problem, let's apply them to a case study that we can use as a working model for the general process. I'll set up a hypothetical organization and a hypothetical software product and walk through the thinking, general problem solving, and overall process to arrive at a compelling interaction model.

Company X

Let's assume that we have a client called Company X, which already has an established desktop application that is fairly successful in their little corner of the market. Company X recognizes that in order to grow their business, they need to break into the mobile market with an iPhone application. On top of that, their users and their investors have been pressuring them to get something into the App Store as soon as possible.

The company has come to you—interaction designer extraordinaire—to help them design their application. They explain to you the need to make a big splash in the App Store. One of their main competitors just released an iPhone App, and Company X needs to release to market a superior application.

Company X focuses on entertainment, and their desktop application allows users to browse and consume content from many different sources. For the most part the content consists of videos, but there are audio files and still images that need to be accounted for too. Company X takes great pride in their ability to curate and organize the content in their application so that their users can easily find what they are looking for. It's what sets them apart from the competition.

However, Company X has a problem: while their desktop application looks great and performs well for users, it cannot be easily translated to an iPhone app. There are just too many controls, buttons, and other user interface widgets, all of which are oriented for mouse and cursor interaction. Adding to the complexity of the user experience is that fact that there are way too many options for navigating the content. For the most part the hierarchy of organization is three tiers deep, but you have noticed several exceptions that go a few layers deeper.

Company X's Requirements

With this knowledge in place you can begin to tackle the design problem. As I reviewed earlier, the first step in the processes is about getting definition around the requirements for what the application needs to be able to do. After reviewing Company X's desktop application and interviewing the key stakeholders for this project you learn that the iPhone app needs to do the following things:

- Give users access to the company's complete library of content.

- Provide a mechanism for users to quickly and efficiently browse and discover new content.

- Allow users to share content with their friends.

- Allow users to comment on content.

- Provide a mechanism for users to add their own content—captured or created on their iPhone—to Company X's library to be shared with the world.

Through the process of gathering requirements and the subsequent discussions with stakeholders, the team concludes that these are the right features to showcase in the iPhone app. And while this doesn't represent all the functionality available from the desktop application, understanding the desires of the user through the personas and scenarios specific to the mobile context helps you filter everything down to these basic features.

Now that you have these requirements in place, you can start thinking through how to organize the workflow for this app. To fully appreciate the possibilities enabled by interaction modeling, it's worth spending some time getting into the details of how to arrive at your workflow definition and how far it needs to be developed.

Reviewing Company X's requirements for the iPhone app reveals something significant about the nature of the app. The vast majority of the requirements relate directly to browsing and consuming content. Ancillary features like sharing and commenting are directly dependent on there being content on screen for users to take action on. So you come to the conclusion that content is the central component to this user experience, and as such the relationship between content and the basic functionality of the app needs to be considered very carefully. Furthermore, in your discussions with the client you are getting a sense of the difficulty of the design problem. The vast majority of the interaction performed by the user focuses on navigating through hierarchical tiers of organization to get to the content.

This is where things get a bit subjective. You can decide to include the hierarchical nature of the content organization and the required path that the user needs to take, or you can simplify that aspect of the workflow and isolate the browsing feature to a single node. Let's take a quick look at the difference with a simple workflow reflecting what we understand about Company X's requirements (see Figure 6-13):

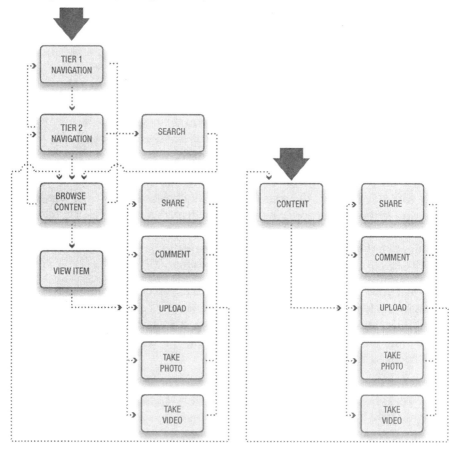

Figure 6-13. An explicit workflow compared to one that has been simplified

This presents an interesting question: What is the rationale for being more explicit or less explicit in your workflow documentation? You always want to create explicit workflows when a user's path through an application has a direct impact on your design decisions at the user interface level. If you know that the inherent structure of your workflow may be simplified by your design decisions at the user interface level, then it makes sense to collapse those details to a single node and not worry about including those details at the workflow level.

In the case of Company X's iPhone app, there is a requirement to provide a mechanism for users to quickly and efficiently browse and discover new content. So you know that at some point you are going to need to resolve the issue of hierarchy with a solution that is more appropriate for an iPhone. For the purposes of this application it makes sense to collapse browsing and content viewing down to single node (see Figure 6-14). This begins to make more sense when we start to think through possible interaction models. With that said, let's use this basic workflow to guide our modeling efforts.

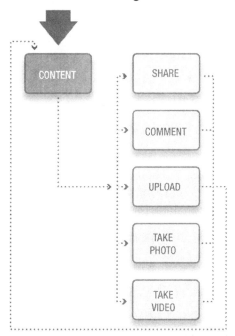

Figure 6-14. Collapsing navigation to a single node knowing that the explicit navigation through a hierarchy may be simplified.

With this basic workflow now in hand, we understand that one of the biggest design challenges for Company X is to figure out how to get users to the content in a way that makes sense for an iPhone app. This is where our interaction modeling activities come into play.

Application Details

To better understand the nature of content browsing, you decide to investigate Company X's desktop application in more detail. You see that they guide the user through the browsing process by providing some general top-tier categories, about ten in total. Within each of these top-tier categories there are about 100 subcategories. Once you select a subcategory you can see the content objects, which from what you can tell, number in the thousands.

The interaction model used by the desktop application is very straightforward. You are presented with a grid of options where each major category is represented in a unit of the grid. Selecting a category refreshes the grid with subcategory items. Selecting a subcategory refreshes the grid with content objects that you can continue to browse visually, at which point you can navigate through multiple pages of content objects contained with that subcategory.

You also notice that the application manages navigation through this space somewhat awkwardly. There is a notion of global navigation, but it only appears when you are at least one layer deep in the experience. When diving down to the content level, you only have access to the top-level categories. It looks to you like a major oversight that a user It looks to you like a major oversight that a user It looks to you like a major oversight that a user . On top of that, there's a lack of context for the user at the content level; when browsing content objects it's not obvious which subcategory you are in.

It's important to note that when you go through a process like this, where you are reviewing an existing application or some other user experience, you should remember to take the time to document your observations and thoughts. Your notes may go a long way toward informing the development of the new interaction model. As we saw with our experiment in early part of this chapter, even a seemingly insignificant seed of a thought can be expanded into a much larger concept without too much effort. In some cases you may want to include some of your foundational thinking as derived from these observations in your interaction modeling documentation to support the ideas you may be presenting.

For the purposes of this case study, you would want to make special note of the nature of Company X's content hierarchy since that will likely have a significant impact on the nature of your solution. So, after reviewing the app you get a sense that their content structure can be understood like this (see Figure 6-15):

TIER 1	**CATEGORIES**	TENS OF ITEMS
TIER 2	**SUBCATEGORIES**	HUNDREDS OF ITEMS
TIER 3	**CONTENT OBJECTS**	THOUSANDS OF ITEMS

Figure 6-15. Company X's content structure & its implications for object browsing

This seems to be an accurate representation of the overall structure. You notice that one of the fundamental issues with the current interaction model is that the user must always back out of the third tier of the hierarchy to get back to sub-categorical, or categorical navigation. That just doesn't seem right. But that's only the tip of the iceberg. You're still not sure if this grid model is even valid for an iPhone experience, but given the visual nature of the navigation model you give it a shot.

Given that we've already conceptualized a grid concept, let's take a stab at recycling that concept. Let's use the same mechanics of interaction that we tried before and just apply that to the concept of moving through a hierarchy (see Figure 6-16).

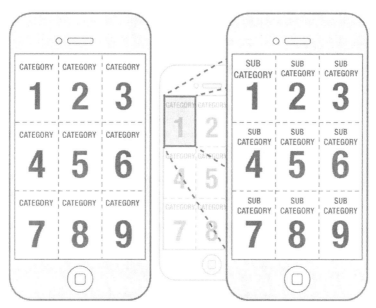

Figure 6-16. Grid concept showing navigation to tier 2 objects

This model has a very close relationship to the existing application experience with its explicit use of a grid of objects. This may be of benefit to users who are already familiar with the desktop application. However, in this model we have to contend with the constraints of the platform, particularly screen size, so we have limited the main view to a two-by-two configuration. In the desktop application the grid is ten by at least 15, depending on how wide you make your application window.

Like the other example that we created, this model could support a spread gesture or a basic tap to navigate down through the categories. In this case we'll use the idea of an expansion threshold a bit differently. Instead of having that threshold relatively high to create an intermediary state, we want the threshold of expansion to be very low. As soon as the system interprets the gesture, we want to transition to the next category.

The key to this interaction model is the visual transitions presented as the user moves through the hierarchy. We want the content to feel as if it is nested within its subcategory, and subcategories nested within their top-level category. As you spread open a unit you will see the underlying content emerge and fill the space. It's very much a direct representation of how information is organized within the app, and it goes a long way toward presenting a very clear model to the user.

Unfortunately this model has a few issues, the least of which concerns navigation back up the hierarchy. It's possible that you could use a reverse gesture to navigate back up a tier, but that seems untidy and awkward to say the least. So while this concept has the potential for some very interesting visual interaction, the interactions don't map well to the needs of the app. In other words, the solution is not extensible; this is one of the big red flags we need to keep our eyes out for.

The other concern is that the model represents a two-handed solution, meaning that the user would have to hold the phone with one hand and use the free hand to navigate the app. This isn't necessarily a bad thing, but given the context of mobility that we are ultimately designing for, it's not an ideal solution.

So what other alternatives can we work through? Let's take a step back again and think through the possibilities of a list. Lists are very convenient for one-handed control, and they can be structured to manage the navigation through hierarchical tiers very simply. This fact makes their use on the iPhone almost a universally applicable solution, but it would be a solution that represents a very low degree of differentiation. Is there a different way to treat this new list concept?

We pushed the list concept to the extreme before, so maybe this time we can be a bit more literal and figure out a way to include some additional value. We don't need to differentiate just for the sake of being different, at least not when there are still issues that we need to address. The previous interaction model didn't support navigation back up the hierarchy effectively, so that's something that we'll want to address this time. There was also the issue of categorical context observed in the desktop application; that is, it was hard to determine where you were, not to mention the fact that you had to back all the way out to the top level to dive into another category. Let's walk through a model that may address these issues.

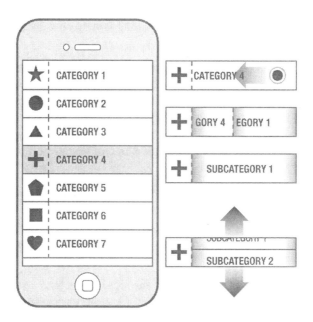

Figure 6-17. A typical list with unique interactions. The user can swipe left to reveal a list of tier 2 objects hidden under the original list element.

Ok, we have a solution here that at first glance appears to be a fairly straightforward list of categories that can be browsed by scrolling up and down. However, this one departs from the standard iOS list treatment in many ways. Navigation through the first two tiers is managed within the same basic view. If a user selects a list element, instead of navigating to another screen, the next tier of subcategories is revealed within the list element itself (see figure 6-17). So basically we just implemented a state change to the list item to expose another tier of navigation within the available area. A user can scroll within that region to browse the subcategories, while context is maintained by the category label that appears above the region. At the same time the user still has visibility of and access to the top-level categories.

Triggering the state change to the list element could be accomplished with a deliberate swipe to the left directly on the list item itself, or we could designate a discrete target to trigger the reveal animation that displays the subcategories. If we decide to implement this design it would be worth exploring both options to get a sense of which interaction feels more natural and which is less prone to user error.

This model presents a very efficient browsing technique, with the main benefit of providing a user access to the first two tiers in the hierarchy simultaneously, but there are some significant challenges here as well. Constraining the browsing of subcategories to a smaller portion of the screen is not inherently efficient, especially if we can only see a maximum of two items at a time. To add to that, this particular model only addresses navigation to the subcategory level; the content tier would need to use another model that could leverage the maximum amount of real estate. So again, this solution may not be viable for Company X's application.

Is there a way to deliver the same level of navigational flexibility to the user, while allowing for the greater prominence of the available content? The previous design solution also uses a disproportionate amount of real estate to display the top-level categories, which feels a bit counterintuitive. And let's also try to shoot for a solution that provides convenient one-handed access. Remember, the requirement states that we need to provide the user with a means to quickly and efficiently browse their content.

Let's continue to work with the list concept, but this time let's think about adding some different properties to the list that may make browsing a bit more fluid. In this case, there isn't a notion of a discrete state change on the screen. It's a more dynamic solution that is responsive to interaction from the user.

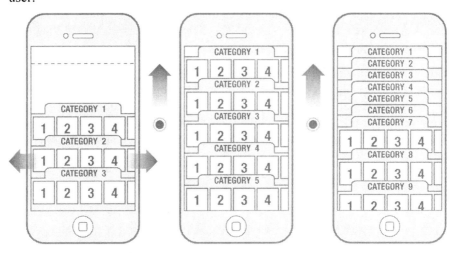

Figure 6-18. Combining tier 1 & tier 2 objects to provide faster access to content. A user scrolls vertically through tier 1 and horizontally through tier 2.

This concept is a bit different from the others in that in its initial state we reserved some space for both dedicated navigation and the other core functionality that needs to be accounted for. You'll notice that I do not illustrate those particular features in the model. The reason for this is straightforward: an interaction modeling exercise does not and should not need to demonstrate all details of the application. The main purpose of the effort is to help you begin to formulate the high-level interactions that will form the basis of your application experience. With that in mind, you need to focus your efforts on resolving content browsing first, while providing high-level considerations for the ancillary interactions.

This model begins with an initial state that displays a limited amount of top-level categories, leaving room for a utility region that will come in handy when we map out the rest of the user interface later in the project. Top-level categories are only treated as a labels in this model, giving users immediate access to second-tier organization. User can quickly move among all top-level categories while viewing the second level (see Figure 6-18). This gives users nonlinear access to all categorical organization.

Exposing additional categories from the initial state of the app only requires a user to scroll the array of objects to the top of the screen. As the categories reach their boundary limit on the screen they collapse to make room for the display of additional categories. The user does not have to take any direct action to cause a category to collapse; categories will collapse automatically based on their position on the screen. The effect is something like the bellows on an accordion.

Content browsing at the subcategory level maps nicely to this model too. When the user selects a subcategory in the first view, they are transitioned to grid of content that can either support additional content categorization like we see in the top level, or an unlabeled grid (see Figure 6-19). Viewing content only requires the user to make a selection on the grid, at which point they are taken to a full-screen view of the content.

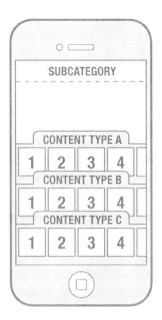

Figure 6-19. In this model, content can be exposed with a single touch.

Navigation back up the hierarchy is managed at the top of the screen. For the purposes of this model it could be as simple as a back button, or as complex as a breadcrumb trail. The important thing is, from the perspective of an interaction model, that we have a mechanism to account for navigation controls.

With this solution in hand, we can now go back to the key stakeholders at Company X and walk them through this model. The interaction model documentation does an excellent job explaining the benefits of these interactions from a user's perspective, and at the same time demonstrates how this application can be differentiated from the competition. This is all accomplished without having to produce detailed wireframes, design mockups, or functional prototypes.

Now that you understand the basic process, and have seen what it can enable, please work through some concepts on your own and see where it takes you.

Summary

Wow Factor

Achieving a sense of Wow for your application means that you are attempting to produce a design solution that evokes a specific response from the user. That response can be defined as the point at which the user's engagement with your app exceeds a critical emotional threshold. There are three basic objectives that your design must satisfy to ensure that the emotional threshold is crossed. These are as follows:

- **Immediacy of impact:** A design must be able to elicit an immediate response from the user.

- **Recognition of novelty or identifiable difference:** A user must be able to recognize the novelty of a given design, or at least identify it as being different from a more conventional experience.

- **Positive response:** There must be an inherent appeal to the solution that mitigates the shock of a potentially strange or foreign experience.

Those objectives can be achieved when your design executes well on at least one of these three attributes:

- **Appearance:** This describes the cosmetic attributes of a given design solution as expressed through the screen structure, layout, rendering, and other elements comprising the static-state visuals of an app.

- **Interaction mechanics and behavior:** This refers to the physical interaction or unique gestures and other actions required to engage with the user interface elements of an application.

■ **Visual interaction, motion, and animation:** These refer to the reactive or dynamic elements of a design solution that bring it to life. These may be closely associated with a particular interaction mechanic or behavior by way of feedback or reactivity to user input, but they also account for ambient qualities within a design or even transitory states not directly related to an interaction.

It's possible to achieve your goal by focusing on just one attribute, but you are more likely to have success by striving to address all three.

Interaction Modeling

Interaction modeling is a method by which you can formulate fundamental interaction mechanics and key visual interactions that will serve as the basis for your application experience. This can be broken down into four key linear activities, where the first three activities must be established before continuing with the interaction modeling itself.

■ **Requirement definition**

■ **Use-case and/or scenario development**

■ **Application workflow**

■ **Interaction modeling**

It can be a challenge to create a highly differentiated interaction model, but there are some basic techniques to make the process more productive.

■ **Abstract:** Reduce known interactions, user interface widgets, and other interactive components to their base-level logic.

■ **Reformulate and reapply:** Use the base-level logic to reformulate a visual interaction and explore how that can be put to use by your application.

■ **Validate:** Explore the validity of that interaction against an existing workflow.

- **Resolve:** Address any conceptual conflict and interaction limitations of your interaction by thinking through alternative mappings to space, time, and state, and modify them accordingly.

- **Extend:** Look for means by which your interaction can be extended across all functional areas of your application.

- **Record:** Document your thought process and notate your explorations extensively.

- **Repeat:** Repeat the process until you are satisfied.

- **Document:** Create clear documentation that describes and visually illustrates your emerging interaction model.

Control Mapping and Touchscreen Ergonomics

Touchscreens are certainly much more commonplace than they were a few years ago, but even with their mainstream adoption there is still a lack of understanding as to how to properly account for the physical interaction with these devices. There are many apps out there that have very cool features, but which are so poorly designed from an ergonomic perspective that it astounds me. These apps might seem intriguing enough to download, but are so awkward and uncomfortable to use that they will quickly be deleted off the user's device. Don't let that happen to you! It's worth spending some time reviewing a few basic considerations to keep in mind when designing for an iPhone or iPad. If you take the time to understand the ideas outlined in this chapter, you'll have a solid foundation for making the right design decisions moving forward.

Awareness of Physicality

Much that has been reviewed in this book so far has been concerned with creating breakthrough ideas and concepts, but this chapter diverges from those concerns to address some basic principles that will help ensure the success of your application.

Many of you may be designing for the mobile space for the first time, but are otherwise fairly experienced in application design in other environments. Apart from a comprehensive understanding of input and output constraints, designing for mobile devices means that you have to be aware of the physicality and kinesiology associated with the manipulation of these devices. If you have designed or developed for the Web, or designed client-side applications, I would imagine that you never gave a thought to how a user's physical interaction with the input devices would affect your design. This is because the interaction with desktop systems is largely taken for granted. The basic format of keyboard, display, and mouse hasn't changed much at all in the past 30 years. Those are essentially fixed hardware inputs that you have had little or no control over, so there was certainly no need to account for the ergonomics of the mouse while worrying about the workflow of your application.

Transitioning to mobile devices requires you to expand your design thinking beyond traditional boundaries. Instead of using fixed hardware inputs to control an application, we now have a situation where we can manifest controls in virtual environment with a high degree of flexibility. The basic input is touch, but that touch can be directed at any number of controls, taking any form, at any location. It's almost as if in addition to your design activities focused on the application, you are now responsible for redesigning the keyboard and mouse—for every application you create! This opens up a lot of options to you as a designer, and not all of those options are good.

iPhone

The iPhone's smaller-scale form factor is easily held in hand. It is the essence of contemporary mobile computing. A user can hold the device and manipulate all of the hard controls with one hand. Much thought went into the placement of the four buttons and one switch that constitute the physical controls on the device. The placement of those hard controls suggests that there is only one primary modality for holding the device, although we know that actually isn't the case.

Given the fact that you are trying to create a differentiated interaction model, there's a good chance that you could arrive at a potential solution that meets all of your objectives, but is ultimately uncomfortable or impractical to use. There are six basic grip patterns, shown in Figures 7-1 to 7-6, for an iPhone that you always want to consider when designing your app. This doesn't mean that your application layout needs to account for each one of these, though that would be great if it could. It just means that your design should work well with at least one grip in mind.

Figure 7-1. One handed vertical iPhone use.

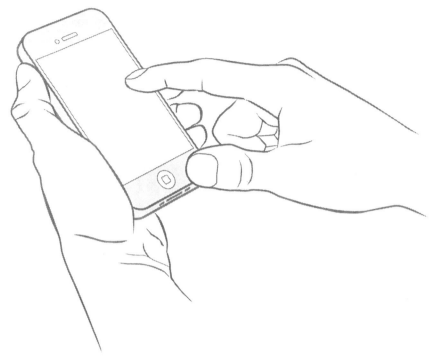

Figure 7-2. Vertical iPhone use with a free hand.

Figure 7-3. Vertical iPhone use with two hands.

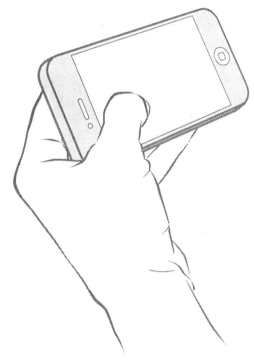

Figure 7-4. One handed horizontal iPhone use.

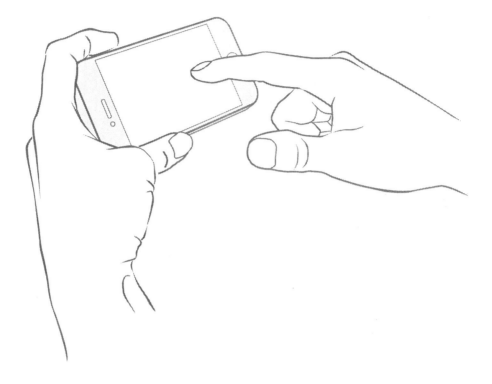

Figure 7-5. Horizontal iPhone use with a free hand.

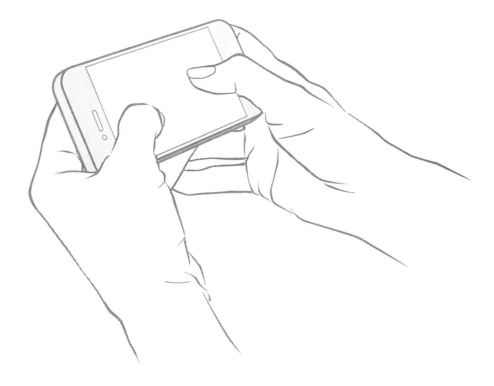

Figure 7-6. Horizontal iPhone use with two hands.

Obviously there are more ways to hold and interact with an iPhone than just the six positions outlined here, but I believe these six are representative of the most likely scenarios that you can expect to encounter. Each of these grips may influence the placement of controls or how you decide to structure the mechanics of a gesture. The position of the user's hands and the orientation of the device can make a huge difference in the overall efficiency of an interaction. Experiment early and often with all of these different positions to get an understanding of how they might influence or alter your design solution.

iPad

The iPad presents a slightly different situation when it comes to physical interaction. An iPad is significantly larger than an iPhone, and as I reviewed in Chapter 4, it's targeted toward a different use-case that likely contributed significantly to determining its final form factor. We know that the iPad is focused more on a leisure-oriented computing experience. That type of experience often requires longer periods of engagement on the part of the user. This gives us the following scenario to contend with:

- It's a larger device.
- It's used for longer periods of time.

These two factors imply that there are very few scenarios where an iPad will be used with just one hand. I'm not saying that it's impossible to use with one hand, especially if it's resting on a surface, but all of the two-handed scenarios are much more relevant. Let's take a look at what those are in Figures 7-7 to 7-10:

Figure 7-7. Vertical iPad use with a free hand..

Figure 7-8. Vertical iPad use with two hands.

Figure 7-9. Horizontal iPad use with a free hand.

Figure 7-10. Horizontal iPad use with two hands.

As with the iPhone, be cognizant of your control positioning relative to how a user may be handling the device.

Basic Layout Considerations

I touched briefly on the ideas of scale and proximity in Chapter 2, but since this is such an important topic it's worth reviewing in greater detail so you can make an informed decision about the layout of your user interface and how you manage the presentation of controls. Just to clarify, when I say control, I'm referring to any interactive object that appears on the screen of an iOS device.

There are two basic factors you need to take into consideration when designing any touch-based control:

- **Scale:** The size of the target area for the control that you are designing.

- **Proximity:** How close that control is to the other user interface elements surrounding it.

These ideas apply equally to both the iPhone and the iPad and are somewhat independent of display resolution. I say "somewhat" because the overall resolution density of the iPad and iPhone is high enough that resolution isn't really a factor anymore.

So we have these two basic concerns, target size and target proximity. Before the iPhone era, I would be making some pretty explicit recommendations about the size of your touch targets. Up until just a few years ago it was conventional wisdom up that touch targets could not be smaller than a specific minimum size without causing significant usability issues for the user. This minimum size was usually quoted to be something between 1 cm^2 to 1.5 cm^2. If you think about it, that's a pretty big button, bigger than the app icons in iOS. To add to this, it was often recommended that touch targets be spaced apart by that same minimal area as well; in other words, spaced with a minimum gap of 1 cm on each axis. There was a reason for this. The technologies that drove some of the older touchscreen systems were not all that accurate. In many cases, the mechanism sensing touch was offset spatially from the actual display itself. To have a usable system you had to account for all kinds of possible discrepancies, including misaligned touch sensors and the parallax associated with an offset surface. Adding to that was the concern that users needed the psychological assurance of larger controls that appeared comfortably touchable.

Luckily we don't have to deal with all that anymore. However, you still want to be considerate of scale and proximity so as not to create too many challenges for the user. Scale is not so much an issue unto itself. The capacitive technology used in iOS devices is highly accurate and highly resolved. You've probably noticed this when browsing the Web on your iPhone. Even without enlarging the view, you can still tap those tiny little links on a web page with the edge of your pinkie finger. So I don't necessarily want to be dogmatic about the minimum size of a touch target, at least not in a vacuum. The key to this is the understanding of proximity.

Proximity is important just for the fact that the closer touch targets are to one another, the greater the chance of error on the part of the user. I think that's pretty much common sense. But again, I don't think we need to get dogmatic about spacing distance either because I don't believe absolute values are useful or even relevant, for that matter.

Here's how you need to think about control spacing:

■ **The spacing between touch targets should be inversely proportional to the size of the adjacent targets (see Figure 7-11).**

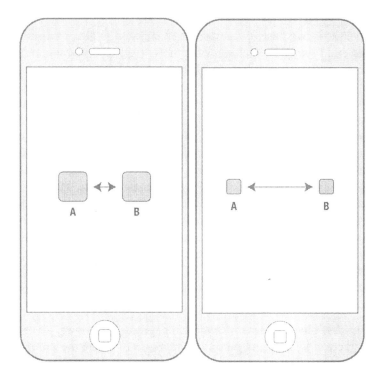

Figure 7-11. The spacing between touch targets should be inversely proportional to the size of the adjacent targets.

That is, the greater the size of your touch targets, the closer they can be grouped together. Conversely, as your touch targets get smaller, they should be spaced farther apart. Smaller targets are more difficult to hit, and when mapped together in a dense configuration they will be prone to user error.

Large targets are easy to hit, so they can be spaced closer together with less risk of user error.

So have at it: make a button as big a single pixel, just know that it may be the only button on the screen when all is said and done!

Feedback and Reactivity

I want to add a few points about timing and reactivity as they may be applied to the interactions in your design. I already reviewed how the concept of time can be applied to resolve potential design problems and why animation is always an important consideration. But in this case I'll be getting into a bit more detail about how to think about the response to input.

Providing users with effective feedback for their system input is fundamental to any thorough design solution. Feedback confirms that an event has taken place, and that the system has captured the event. Typically this takes the form of simple state changes applied to the graphics that represent the point of interaction for any given control. In this sense, feedback serves a very pragmatic purpose that is valid in any interactive context.

However, feedback presents another point of design differentiation that can add a layer of emotional engagement to an app when approached in the right way. So apart from the differentiated approach to your interaction model, be sensitive to the unit-level interactions embedded in the model itself. What I mean by this is that you still need to be aware of how the details of a specific interaction, like the touch of a button, affect your overall design solution.

One of the most common complaints I hear from designers who are transitioning into the mobile space for the first time is the lack of an "over" or "hover" state. Designers see this as an issue because over presents some interesting creative possibilities. The thing is, over is just a feedback mechanism and there are plenty of opportunities to incorporate elegant and creative feedback elsewhere. Let's just think about the most basic event in a touch-screen scenario: the touch itself. For the most part, the conventional approach to feedback on a touch event is just to do a simple state change in the appearance of the control. I think the lack of creative thinking beyond the basic appearance swap is a holdover from previous technologies where the "mouse down" or "mouse click" event superseded any other system activity, thereby limiting the visual interaction that could occur. iOS exacerbates this convention by making state an inherent attribute of the control itself, allowing for the easy implementation of basic feedback.

The idea of touch in the real world implies reaction and feedback. We live in world governed by well-established physical laws. We should look to our experience in the world to inform the nature of reactivity in our interface designs. Knowing this, there is much more that can be applied to the touch event on the device to either add realism or interest for the user. Not only can we change the appearance of a control, we have the capability to change that appearance over time as well. Are there animated reactions to your unit-level interactions that you can apply to your design? Sure there are. Can we provide visual feedback, in real time, for our contact points on the screen while performing gestures? Of course.

If you plan to integrate more robust feedback and reactivity into you designs, always be sensitive to timing. Timing refers to how quickly an event is triggered, how quickly it is displayed, and the duration of the displayed effect. These are all very important factors because you need to be aware of how an animation or effect may impact the overall flow of a task. If a user has to wait for a sequence to finish before the system transitions to the next point in the workflow, then there is chance that the user may get frustrated. Like anything else, there can be a fine line between frustration and engagement, so always be prepared to refine your solution in order to get this right.

Prompting for Hidden Controls

There are always going to be user interface solutions that require you to actively manage the presentation of controls on screen. I'm referring here to highly state-driven user interfaces where a control set must first be invoked by the user, before they are able to take action on the controls themselves. These types of user interface solutions can be problematic because they hide controls from the user. This seems counterintuitive from a usability perspective, but there are many valid situations where this is useful.

The key to making these types of solutions successful is recognizing that you must provide some kind of prompt of hint for the action that reveals the control. This could be as simple as making all your hidden control sets visible when the app initially launches, making the user aware of their existence, then animating them off screen in some manner. You could even provide the user with explicit instructions in that initial launch state that describes the functions and the interaction required to bring them back onto the screen. This is especially useful for situations where the user is required to perform a specific gesture, rather than just a simple tap on the screen.

When controls are in their hidden state, it may be useful to included a subtle, transparent icon or other visual indicator identifying the location of the control. You have time and state to work with as well, so maybe prompts can appear at critical points in a workflow, or appear at predefined intervals.

Once a user becomes familiar with your app these prompts will not be required, so consider providing some user control within the app or in the Settings application to manage this. Remember to communicate to the user that they can control this, so they don't become frustrated down the road.

Summary

Let's review what you've learned in this chapter on Control Mapping and Touch Screen Ergonomics:

- Always consider the physical attributes of the device that you are designing for and how that may impact the usage of your application.

- Be conscientious of the scale and proximity of your controls as you map them out across your application. The spacing between touch targets should be inversely proportional to the size of the adjacent targets to minimize the possibility of user error.

- There are many ways to integrate dynamic visual feedback into your application. Don't ignore the unit-level interactions; many creative possibilities can be applied at that level.

- If your design solution includes the possibility of hidden controls, always provide a prompting mechanism to communicate the behavior that reveals the control set.

Ease of Use and Feature Automation

This last chapter addresses automation, which I consider a very interesting aspect of user experience design that has emerged over the past few years. The idea of automation is compelling because it actively tries to hide from the user critical details pertaining to the operation of an application. Extensive automation is starting to make its way into all different kinds of consumer applications, and it is an emerging technique that has a high degree of relevance for both the mobile and portable use-cases.

I'll be outlining some basic guidance to help you understand where and how the automation of features can be applied to user experience, and what considerations apply when doing so.

Why Automation?

We are in an era that is seeing significant technological change at an extremely rapid pace. As reviewed in Chapter 3, this is causing a significant shift of user perceptions and user expectations, and for the most part we have seen users become more sophisticated as the market evolves.

One of the emergent trends arising from this is the desire for increased user control in software of all types. This control can occur at a fairly granular level within an app, where there is greater exposure of feature detail, or at a higher level, where users determine what features appear within the app while they use it. In many cases, as the user gains in familiarity and sophistication with the use of an application, they naturally seek more control over the application and to streamline their workflow. From a user experience perspective, interaction designers often find themselves exposing a greater degree of user-definable parameters within applications to address users' increased desire for control.

However, this is just one end of the spectrum. At the other end of the spectrum is the situation where increased amounts of automation work behind the scenes to vastly simplify—or at least clarify—our interaction with technology. In the never-ending quest to make products easier to use, automation stands to be the apotheosis of interaction design, wherein interaction fades into the background as the system assumes more control. Let's be honest, though; this isn't a universal axiom quite yet.

The increased degree of automation inherent to many iOS applications is directly related to the extremely high technological density of the devices themselves. I say "high technological density" because these devices not only contain all the necessary components for computation and interaction, but also multiple communications technologies. Add to that a vast array of additional input and sensing technologies and you have a device with a very high technological density. When you combine computation and communication with all the other data passing in and out of the device you can begin to do some very interesting things, the least of which is optimizing a workflow for a user.

Throughout this chapter, I'll refer to ancillary technologies in an abstract sense, but it's worth outlining what those technologies are so you can consider how they may impact your user experience. These are as follows:

GPS Satellite Data

- User location in both space and time
- Macro movement, speed, and acceleration over long durations
- Vector of movement

Three-Axis Accelerometer

▦ Device orientation and rotation

▦ Micro movement, speed, and acceleration relative to previous position and at a much more granular level than GPS.

Gyroscopic Sensor

▦ Device orientation

Digital Compass

▦ Device orientation relative the magnetic field of the Earth

▦ Vector of movement

Proximity Sensor

▦ Proximity of objects to the surface of the device

Cameras

▦ Image capture

▦ Video capture

Microphone

▦ Audio capture

To be clear, automation provides a number of distinct benefits to the user, and when done in the right way it can help in getting users to cross the emotional threshold and experience the wow factor of your application.

When It Is Applicable

When I talk about automation in the context of an application I refer to the elimination of discrete steps, tasks, or decision points required of the user to perform a particular workflow. The removal of these elements is done with the intent of simplifying the overall workflow for the user. I think it's safe to say that in general, a simplified workflow is an easier workflow, and "easier" is a goal toward which you should continually strive.

However, a workflow that has been simplified from the user's perspective does not imply that it was simple for the designer to arrive at that solution. From a design perspective it's easy enough to remove a step from a workflow diagram and call it done, but that's not how you go about it.

Automation only becomes applicable when the ancillary sensing and input technologies allow you to make some very educated guesses about a user's intentions with respect to their particular position within a given workflow. In almost all cases, resolving the system assumptions about user behavior is a significantly challenging technical task—so much so that it may not be worth doing. It's up to you, as the interaction designer, to work closely with your developers and engineers to identify points in your workflow that may be assisted by the ancillary technologies.

How and where this idea is applied to your application should be outlined as a part of your user experience strategy. Be aware that automation can be used in many different ways and at many different levels of a design solution. You may have an application whose fundamental value proposition lies in its ability to display weather information based on the current location of the device, with no user interaction required. In this situation, the idea of automation is fundamental to your value proposition. But you can use automated techniques at a more granular level too. Let's use iOS as an example. A user can hold an iOS device in many different ways (see Chapter 7). As the user changes the orientation of the device, the content viewed reorients and reformats itself automatically to the new orientation. It's automatic.

Let's think about the alternative for a moment. Even without accelerometers or a compass, the reorientation task could be achieved by including an orientation toggle control embedded in the UI. But since we do have the ability to determine orientation, we can make the assumption that when a physical orientation change occurs, a user wishes to view their content in that new view. In this case automation is not a core driver of a value proposition; rather, it's just a single feature that does not require interaction with a specific control.

Apart from critical workflow enhancements, one of the key indicators for the inclusion of automated features is a high degree of functional detail. Again, this is very much a context-oriented issue, but if you are designing for a consumer-based persona that lacks technical sophistication, you will almost always want to reduce the amount of functional detail apparent in your application. For example, if you are designing a camera app, you might have the technical ability to expose ISO settings and aperture control at a very granular level. That's great, but the end user targeted by this app may be unfamiliar with the operation of these settings. In this situation you may want to think about collapsing functionality to predetermined presets that may be applicable to common photography scenarios. To take this a step further, you may want to look for ways to automate the activation of presets based on environmental factors and the nature of imagery being captured by the camera.

As always, the mobile context of iPhone usage should provide you with the lens to help shape your design decisions. Being on the go, multitasking, and leveraging impulsive behavior all suggest a very streamlined approach to your presentation of functionality. In addition to that, the iPhone lacks the physical real estate required expose a high degree of functional density. So it's likely you would want to bias toward more automation whenever possible.

The iPad's larger form factor and associated usage patterns suggest that a different mentality is likely relevant, but your prerogative as an interaction designer should always lead you to more elegant solutions that will likely include enhancements enabled by the use of the ancillary sensing technologies.

Keep in mind that network connectivity can play a significant role here as well. Both the iPad and the iPhone have significant computational abilities, but the synthesis of information arriving from the ancillary sensing technologies may be more than app can handle on its own. Connectivity to larger-scale systems may be required for complex automation to occur. Certain actions, such as complex image processing, may need to be offloaded to cloud-based services in order to provide the desired level of performance within the app.

How to Approach Feature Automation

Most of what I have reviewed so far has really only been focused on one approach to the automation of features. This is the situation where we seek opportunities to bypass user control at the appropriate point in a workflow. However, there is a more nuanced approach that may be just as relevant.

To break it down, there are two basic ways to think about the automation of features within your application:

■ Bypassing user control: The outright removal of specific input required of the user based on key assumptions regarding user intent

■ Augmenting user control: The active simplification or active guidance of user control–based key assumptions regarding user intent

Both methods require you to make an explicit analysis in a few key areas to fully understand the degree to which you can automate a feature. Start by looking into these details:

■ The user's workflow position within the application

■ All possible user intent relative to the workflow or task

■ The available data as supplied by the device relative to user intent

■ The data processing required to validate intent or synthesize application results based on known intent

As you can see, these activities are focused on understanding how much you can establish regarding the intent of the user. When intent is known, or when it's feasible to deduce intent, you can apply the appropriate degree of feature automation to your application.

Summary

While application complexity and user sophistication are on the rise, ease of use is still a priority. From an interaction design perspective, it will always make sense to simplify and optimize an interaction, workflow, or application if the opportunity is there. This is especially true for mobile applications, which can benefit significantly from a streamlined approach to their operation.

The abundant technologies available on iOS devices provide an unparalleled amount of data that can be used to help automate many aspects of an application. This can be technically challenging, but the challenge must be weighed against the potential benefit that the automation provides to the user.

Feature automation has the potential to create a high degree of emotional impact. When used in conjunction with differentiated appearance, visual interaction, and behavior, you are almost guaranteed to achieve the wow factor that you seek.

I

Index

A, B

Automation, 125
  augmenting user control, 130
  bypassing user control, 130
  cameras, 127
  digital compass, 127
  GPS satellite data, 126
  gyroscopic sensor, 127
  microphone, 127
  proximity sensor, 127
  three-axis accelerometer, 127
  workflow, 127–29

C, D, E, F

Carousel view spatial model, 19
Core Animation, 62, 67
Core Graphics, 62, 67

G

Gestures, 13–14

H

Human Interface Guidelines (HIG), 1

aesthetic integrity, 5
drawbacks and limitations, 4–5
market fragmentation, 2, 3
memory availability, 2
platform characteristics, 3
processor capability, 2
signature interaction, 3
smartphones, 2
themes, 3

I, J

Interaction modeling, 69
  application workflow, 73
  array of objects, 78
  desktop application, iphone
    entertainment, 92
    global navigation, 96
    Requirements, 93, 95
    reveal concept, 99
    subcategory, 96
    superscrubber concept, 101,
      102
    tier concept, 97
    visual transitions, 99
  documentation, 90–91

CPSIA information can be obtained at www.ICGtesting.com
Printed in the USA
LVOW100903290212

270913LV00009BA/31/P